COUNSELLING COUPLES
AND FAMILIES

COUNSELLING COUPLES AND FAMILIES

A Person-Centred Approach

Charles J. O'Leary

SAGE Publications
London • Thousand Oaks • New Delhi

Excerpt from 'Little Gidding' in *Four Quartets* © 1942 by
T.S. Eliot and renewed 1970 by Esme Valerie Eliot, reprinted
by permission of Harcourt Inc. and Faber & Faber Ltd.

First published 1999

 SAGE Publications Ltd
6 Bonhill Street
London EC2A 4PU

SAGE Publications Inc
2455 Teller Road
Thousand Oaks, California 91320

SAGE Publications India Pvt Ltd
32, M-Block Market
Greater Kailash – I
New Delhi 110 048

British Library Cataloguing in Publication data

A catalogue record for this book is available
from the British Library

ISBN 0 7619 5790 1
ISBN 0 7619 5791 X (pbk)

Library of Congress catalog card number 99–71384

Typeset by Mayhew Typesetting, Rhayader, Powys
Printed in Great Britain by The Cromwell Press Ltd,
Trowbridge, Wiltshire

To Martha Beth, Gwenyth Kate and Emily Grace

Contents

Foreword

Dave Mearns

Dr Charles O'Leary works in Arvada, just outside Denver, exactly midway between the politically contrasting communities of Colorado Springs and Boulder. Charlie is well suited to working with varied communities. Proud of his Boston-Irish background, he combines the humour of that heritage with an acute observation of human behaviour. This is a perfect combination for a family therapist, especially one who commentates upon family therapy through public lectures and now in this book. In his lecturing, Charlie is able to combine his sharpness of wit and observation to bring the client to life in the imaginations of his audience. Furthermore, he achieves that in such a fashion that does not demean the client but accentuates the humanity of all concerned. I believe that he also achieves that in this book.

Charlie has his roots firmly set in the person-centred approach. When I first met him in 1972 we were both graduate students attached to the Center for Studies of the Person (CSP) in La Jolla, California. He had crossed the country to study with Dr Carl Rogers when CSP, in typical near-sixties fashion, had undertaken an unconventional academic programme.

The person-centred approach has always maintained an uneasy relationship with conventional institutions. Some years ago, a prominent voluntary counselling agency in Britain declared that the person-centred approach was inappropriate for couples work because its emphasis was on empowering the individual. Within the person-centred approach the response would be that relationships might be considerably enhanced if the partners gained even a little more power over the matter of their own living. Conversely, if relationships are to be preserved at the expense of human growth, then our humanity may be in terminal decline.

In fact, the person-centred approach articulates well with couple and family therapy. Carl Rogers' 'Self' theory, underlying person-centred work, is entirely 'systemic', to the extent that family therapy concepts can even be applied directly to the configurations and dynamics which operate within the Self (Mearns, 1999). As the person-centred therapist establishes contact with each emerging dimension of Self, she seeks to hold it in relationship while equally honouring other parts which may be in discord, and this is the case with many families.

Within the development of family therapy the parallels with person-centred counselling have been evident. In Chapter 4, Charlie articulates the fundamental nature of the person-centred 'core conditions' to family therapy. Indeed, sometimes we see therapists sharpening essentially person-centred ideas in their translation into family work. A prime example is the vibrant concept of 'multi-directional partiality' coined by Ivan Boszormenyi-Nagy (Boszormenyi-Nagy and Ulrich, 1981). This challenges the family therapist not simply to be passively accepting of each family member, but to be experienced by *every* family member as 'partial' to them. Person-centred therapists will find their conception of 'unconditional positive regard' stretched by this kind of translation into family work. Indeed, that is what comes over well in this book – the picture of the family therapist being very *active* and stretched to engage fully with every person in the family.

While the book will be useful in helping couple and family therapists to see the relationship between their work and the person-centred approach, it will be invaluable to the person-centred therapist who is considering developing their couple and family work. Chapter 2, 'Why Do Counsellors Stay Away from Relational Counselling?', anticipates and discusses their fears, Chapter 5 helps them to prepare for relational counselling and Chapters 6, 7 and 8 follow the structure of the popular series 'Counselling in Action', also published by Sage, by taking the reader through the process of 'beginnings', 'middles' and 'endings' of the therapeutic process.

As would be expected by anyone who has been to a Charlie O'Leary lecture or workshop, the book is crammed full of illustrative material from couples and families, making it is a thoroughly good read for even the casual reader. I commend this book to the reader, whoever who are!

Introduction

Many person-centred counsellors are seeking to learn more about couples and family counselling. Helpful individual counselling often stimulates clients' desire to involve partners, children and even parents in what has been one of their most significant life experiences. Further, since individual therapy often causes change in relationships, some counsellors and clients wonder if this journey of personal learning might not better take place in the presence of a partner rather than alone with a therapist. Sometimes therapeutic work on a relationship with parents or siblings raises the possibility of a meeting with such persons in the presence of a facilitator. Person-centred counsellors employed by agencies or in medical practice settings are often called upon to work with people having relationship difficulties. People ask, 'Will you see my husband and me?' When counsellors work with children, they often desire or are asked to meet with the child's family as well. Person-centred counsellors also hear about couples and family therapy attempted unsatisfactorily from other points of view and wonder if in a less directive, interpretive or didactic environment it might have gone better.

In this book, the reader will find my own active dialogue between the person-centred approach and the many ways of thinking and acting which make up the collective literature on marriage and family therapy or 'relational counselling', to use a relatively new term (Anderson, 1997). The term 'relational counselling' encompasses both couples and family counselling. 'Couples counselling' will refer to work with any two adults in an intimate relationship and the term 'family counselling' will describe work when more than two family members are included.

I have been offering workshops on relational counselling for person-centred counsellors for over ten years. In every workshop, participants reveal a desire for work with their own families of origins as well as with their spouses. People who, in person-centred groups, develop the habit of expressing their thoughts and feelings directly, would like to continue that at home without being seen as a threat, an eccentric or a bore. They reveal a longing to attempt the same deep connection that they find in the groups with mothers, fathers, sisters or brothers. They want a setting in which their family members can listen to their truest voice without feeling attacked, threatened or diminished.

I am writing this book because I believe that person-centred counsellors are particularly well prepared to undertake work with couples and families. Proficient person-centred counsellors will have developed that strong sense of self-sufficiency which enables them to 'make themselves small' (Friedman, 1991) thus creating a large thera-peutic space essential for mutual support and challenge between members of a couple or family. Furthermore, person-centred coun-sellors have learned how to communicate their understanding of each family member in an atmosphere of acceptance, thus creating for each person the unique experience of being understood yet not judged in the presence of other family members.

However, I do not want person-centred therapists to attempt relational counselling based *only* on their experiences in counselling individuals or through participating in groups. Family therapy is a *medium* which must be respected on its own terms. It is not individual therapy done one by one with other people present. It is not group therapy or encounter group work where people can engage and then detach without concern about consequences in the atmosphere of their home or bedroom that very night. Family or couples counselling almost always has at least one person who is less engaged, less comfortable and more in the dark about the process of counselling. The relational counsellor must be congruent while learning how to welcome reluctant or uncomfortable participants. Family therapist Jay Haley spoke of this need to suspend one's habitual perspective when he said, 'It is rude to be warm to a cold person' (Haley, 1982). The power dynamic is more complex when dealing with a family than with an individual or a group of non-related people. In family work, for example, there is both opportunity and challenge to see such phenomena as 'conditions of worth' in action (Rogers, 1959). The counsellor is asked to relate simultaneously and with acceptance to a person who feels controlled by someone else *and* to the person who feels the need to exert such control!

This book will also raise important questions for every reader about how counselling changes when the dimension of active family relationship is added. Can we add without subtracting? Can we be responsive to the specific medium of family work without losing the unique values of the person-centred approach? I do not want to water down family counselling in order to make it compatible with the person-centred approach. It would, similarly, dilute the power of the person-centred approach to suggest that all, or even most, contemporary family therapy techniques are necessarily compatible with the person-centred approach. In revealing the criticisms that each approach might make of the other, I do not want to be sim-plistic. Good counsellors doing the best they can for their clients, practice these approaches and inevitably emphasize one side of human experience over another. I hope to lay different ways of counselling side by side so that each counsellor can find models from which to choose when meeting the clients who come to the office or clinic.

This book is one of many possible dialogues between principles of the person-centred approach and the activity called relational counselling. It is *personal* and *descriptive* rather than *comprehensive* or *prescriptive*. I have chosen to write this book as a series of reflections about the way in which the person-centred approach already enlivens the best of relational counselling. Many examples I give are drawn from the work of counsellors who do not identify themselves as person-centred. I have interviewed several practising family and couples counsellors in preparation for this work and will quote them throughout the book. I also reflect on ways in which the style of a person trained in person-centred individual therapy would be very effective in relational counselling, as well as the ways in which a counsellor may need to adapt. This is a contribution to a long series of reflections on the application of the person-centred approach to work with couples and families including Barrett-Lennard (1984, 1998), Gaylin (1989, 1993), Ellinwood (1989), Anderson (1989a, 1989b), Cain (1989), Levant (1984), Raskin and Van der Veen (1970), Bozarth and Shanks (1989), Snyder (1989), Thayer (1982), Warner (1983, 1989), Guerney (1984), Mearns and Thorne (1988), Mearns (1994a) and Rogers (1961c, 1972a, 1972b).

Like many writers before me (for example Mearns and Thorne, 1988), I do not think there is an exact or useful distinction between the words 'therapy' and 'counselling'. I will use the word 'counselling' predominantly, although when quoting or discussing other writers, I will use the word 'therapy' if they do. I have approached the personal pronoun dilemma by alternating he and she, him and her whenever possible.

I would like to thank many counsellors, writers and friends who lent their energy and talents to this work. The great heroes of this book are Dave Mearns, my talented and thorough editor and friend, who in a supreme act of unconditional positive regard suggested this book and shepherded it into existence; John K. Wood, my thoughtful and persistent friend who lent his considerable understanding of the person-centred approach to help shape my thinking and this book; and finally my wife, Martha Johns, who was an indispensable support, inspiration, and imaginative and loving editor. Breffni Barrett, Eliot Weinstein, David Sanders and Ron Urone are generous and excellent therapists who each submitted to several interviews. Other friends who contributed clinical and literary wisdom or other support include Gay Swenson Barfield, Steven Bennett, Norm Chambers, Larry Chamow, Karen Dinan, Janet Elisita, Katie Elsbree,

Phil Elsbree, Dick Farson, Harry Johns, Molly Johns, Ralph Keyes, Elke Lambers, Bob Lee, Elias Lefferman, Etta Linton, Susan Lund, Joyce Marx, Jeanne McAlister, Bruce Meador, Milt Miller, Bob Mines, Maureen O'Hara, Kathleen O'Leary, Tom Owen-Towle, George Purvis, George Sargent (much missed since his death early in 1998), Wilson Southam, Linda Terry-Geyer, Brian Thorne, Ferdinand Van der Veen, Katie Webb, Doug Young, Marlyn Young and Alberto Zucconni. I am particularly grateful to three likeable and admirable people who in this book are known as the Clark family.

CHAPTER 1

Relational Counselling and the Person-Centred Approach

Family counselling Rogers-style

In his autobiography, Rogers tells a story which may be seen as a kind of 'origins' narrative for the person-centred approach:

> I had learned to be more subtle and patient in interpreting a client's behavior to him, attempting to time it in a gentle fashion which would gain acceptance. I had been working (at the Rochester Child Guidance Clinic in the 1930s) with a highly intelligent woman whose boy was something of a hellion. The problem was clearly her early rejection of the boy, but over many interviews I could not help her to this insight. I drew her out, I gently pulled together the evidence she had given, trying to help her see the pattern. But we got nowhere. Finally I gave up. I told her that it seemed we had both tried, but we had failed and that we might as well give up our contacts. She agreed. So we concluded the interview, shook hands and she walked to the door of the office. Then she turned and asked, 'Do you ever take adults for counselling here?' When I replied in the affirmative, she said, 'Well I would like some help.' She came to the chair she had left, and began to pour out her despair about her marriage, her troubled relationship with her husband, her sense of failure and confusion, all very different from the sterile 'case history' she had given before. Real therapy began then, and ultimately it was very successful. This incident was one of a number which helped me to experience the fact – only fully realized later – that it is the client who knows what hurts, what directions to go, what problems are crucial, what experiences have been deeply buried. It began to occur to me that unless I had a need to demonstrate my own cleverness and learning, I would do better to rely upon the client for the direction of movement in the process. (Rogers, 1967)

Speaking once in a small group, Rogers seemed to enjoy telling how the boy's problems stopped completely once his mother started to talk about the issues which were on her mind rather than on his.

This tale demonstrates values at the heart of the person-centred approach and is also good family counselling. The reader may reflect on what may be learned from this from a person-centred perspective. The following are some inferences that might be drawn from this case presentation:

- the counsellor failed in so far as he attempted to persuade the client into his view of the situation;
- Rogers was not kept from such failure by his being 'patient and subtle' or by what he 'gently pulled together' – he still was taking the one-up or expert position;
- the counselling began to succeed when he became congruently transparent and directly stated his opinion about what was happening without a judgement of the client or of himself;
- it succeeded for his client when he let go of his role and of his judgement and gave control back to her (by proposing they end the therapy); and
- progress was further in evidence when she spoke of her problems and life as they seemed to *her* and the counsellor, as he stated, relied upon the client for the direction of movement in the process.

This story is also meaningful for person-centred counsellors because it reveals the unique quality of Carl Rogers' therapeutic work. He showed humility in his willingness to admit that he was not getting anywhere, but also a kind of boldness and confidence. He refused to let himself remain stuck in a meaningless role. He thought too much of himself to go through motions when he no longer believed in what he was doing. Instead, he was ready to respond to what the moment brought him. He must have had a highly developed sense of hopefulness about people in order to be willing to allow the woman to sit down again with a different frame of reference. He could easily have hurried her out in order to try the same mistakes on the next client. Instead he had a scientist's openness that eventually allowed her to find the right kind of therapy for herself and allowed him to begin his own revolutionary thinking about the nature of therapeutic change.

'Relational counselling', as it is now practised, might have given Rogers other opportunities to have a positive influence on this family. He might have invited the father to join them, even phoning him specifically to ask him to join in on the family problem solving (see Stanton and Todd (1982) for discussion of counsellor phone calls to reluctant family members.) The boy might have been invited to join his parents and, after being consulted, been free to come in and out of the counselling as he felt ready. In Rogers' case, we have never been told what the psychiatrist who saw the boy alone did while Rogers saw his mother. Was the psychiatrist a good listener with children? Did he have the ability to draw out the boy's pain without the boy feeling abnormal and ashamed by his designation as patient? What if the father had seen Carl Rogers and felt understood about his struggles to succeed in 1930s Rochester, New York? Did the boy have other brothers and sisters who might have come and added their stories to the meetings? Would the parents have learned to relate more empathically to each other in the family meetings? Would they have asked to meet with Rogers without the children to talk about ways their relationship was stuck?

The person-centred approach

The reader may consult Rogers (1961d, 1980), Mearns and Thorne (1988) and Barrett-Lennard (1998) for fuller descriptions of the person-centred approach. In this book the following themes will be taken for granted as characteristic of person-centred counsellors. Observation of their work may reveal that they have developed the following abilities:

- to listen without judgement for the truth of every person's own experience;
- to put aside their agenda or their idea of what is the best way for a client to behave and follow the trail of the client's own ability to evaluate accurately;
- to trust in a *formative directional tendency* at work in often apparently chaotic circumstances;
- to suspend questions and comments in favour of empathic tracking of client meaning;
- to be present in the manner of a fellow human who is committed rather than as an expert who is in charge; and
- to work on self-awareness and transparency in each meeting with clients.

Or perhaps more important is what person-centred counsellors learn *not* to do:

- direct people as to what they should do;
- make interpretations about people's inner motivation;
- respond to people as if they are summed up by any diagnosis;
- favour their own understanding of the problem over the client's; and
- hide behind their role, so that the client is left wondering about their intentions or reactions.

The unique value of the person-centred approach is well expressed in a workshop dialogue with a counselling student working with children whose brother or sister had died. The student wondered if she was even really counselling because all she was doing was 'being there for them – seeing them through'. She was told:

> If it's possible, it's the very best thing you can do because children whose world has been broken will be trying to repair it themselves. You can witness how they do it. If you impose your own way of repair on them, at best they will have to suspend their way of doing it until you are done; at worst they will lose the chance to do the repair.

Person-centred counsellors have been seasoned by the unique experience of the person-centred group. They have had opportunity themselves to become aware of their personal biases, defences, strengths, limitations and effect on others. They most likely have had, at least once, the profound experience of feeling completely understood about a part of their life in which they assumed they would always remain isolated and set apart. They have survived many challenges in group process by persons different from themselves and difficult to like. They have learned that the heart of counselling is their personal presence and their ability to connect with acceptance and understanding. They have learned to trust their own spontaneous reactions to people in such a way that no one would think that they were acting out of a formula. Finally, they have learned how to take a strong, even passionate, position without having to impose it on another.

An introduction to couples and family counselling

People live in relationship. Their problems arise partially from the relationships in which they currently live – the words and actions that bind or divide them in relation to others. However, they also carry within them their internalizations of other people: their self-esteem and self-concept are influenced by how others have acted towards them. Their very opinion about their own bodies is shaped, in large part, by the remembered reactions of other people. Few live in isolation, and even those who do, live in internal dialogue with a world whose avoidance gives definition and purpose to their life.

Our individual clients and group members enter the room under the influence of their present companions and the historical companions who were their family of origin. Relational counsellors want to meet those people. They want to bypass the *described* spouse, partner, child, sister, brother and parent and meet the *real* version if possible. Perhaps more importantly they want to see the original client as she is in the presence of her significant others. For example, a person who describes herself as invisible, passive, unimportant may in the presence of her family show a colourfulness, a flair for impact and the ability to influence that she could never reveal by herself. (The reverse could as easily be true.)

Family and couples counsellors are usually trained in a counselling role that is very different from that of individual person-centred counsellors. Family therapy originated as a challenge to medical theory that saw schizophrenics and other persons with problems as isolated patients whose families were considered immune from the effects of the disease. Family therapists developed an *active* and varied repertoire of interventions designed to involve other family members in unaccustomed self-disclosure and ownership of their own difficulties, and as a result to release the schizophrenic from harmful dehumanizing over-focus (Broderick and Schrader, 1991). For example, family therapist Murray Bowen (1978) used genograms or family trees to chart all of the interlocking events that were also occurring in the wider family system when a child was born or first developed symptoms.

Marital or couples therapy originated earlier than family therapy and always had a teaching function, as has behavioural family therapy with its emphasis on teaching skills to parents (Broderick and Schrader, 1991). Marital therapists have focused on educating couples in effective communication and conflict resolution; dealing with the complexity of gender roles; providing opportunities for frank discussion of sexual differences; and facilitating awareness of the day-to-day adaptation to children, finances, families, ageing, illness and compatibility of likes and dislikes (Stuart, 1980).

Persons trained as family and couples therapists are a diverse group whose membership ranges from those who apply the principles of psychoanalysis in a family group setting (Skynner, 1976) to those who, calling themselves solution-focused, ask questions like 'What is different on the days in which you feel you *are* getting along?' (de Shazer, 1985). The earliest leaders in family therapy were male, with the notable exception of Virginia Satir (Satir, 1964). In 1977 an influential group was formed, called The Women's Project, consisting of Betty Carter, Peggy Papp, Olga Silverstein and Marianne Walters (Carter, 1989, 1992; Walters, 1984; Simon, 1997). These four therapists focused on correcting the overly male perspective of couples and family therapy. They found a tendency to devalue the contribution and perspective of women in families: for example, that a desire for connection was often redefined as control or enmeshment (the blurring of psychological boundaries). In the past 15 years, there has been increased but still limited attention to couples and family counselling for gay and lesbian clients (Brown and Zimmer, 1986; Carl, 1990; Markowitz, 1994; Clark and Serovich, 1997).

Three themes which link the behaviour of many contemporary relational counsellors will be presented in Chapter 3. They are counsellor activity, reframing and asking questions. The next section of this chapter will describe a challenge in all relational counselling: the ability to be a counsellor committed to more than one person at once.

Multi-directional partiality: being on everyone's side

One of my colleagues recently said, in frustration, 'I'm no good at couples work!'. When I asked what she meant, she replied 'I was just furious at Bob. He was just so stuck and doing nothing but projecting. Nothing that Pam or I or you said could budge him'. Like me, like every counsellor I know, she was struggling with the *evaluative tendency* (Rogers, 1961b) which could lead her in this case to act as if Bob were the problem and Pam were his victim. By discussion with another counsellor, she was attempting to return to being on his side even while she remained aware of the effects of his behaviour on his partner.

The relational counsellor is asked to live with a paradox which family therapist Ivan Boszormenyi-Nagy has called *multi-directional partiality*, or being on more than one side at once. He has described this as follows:

> Toward the participants the therapist does not adopt a stance of impartial contemplation of all competing interests. We hold that 'impartiality' or 'neutrality' if it can actually be achieved is an undesirable goal, and its pursuit can be deadening. The therapist is multi-directionally partial, i.e., directing empathy, endorsement, listening to one person, then in turn to that person's adversary . . . (Boszormenyi-Nagy and Ulrich, 1981: 178)

For example, the counsellor is called upon to be present for a teenager who feels overwhelmed by his father's demands; at the same time, she must be present to a father who doesn't want to be a party to his son's avoidance of what, to him, seem to be minimal challenges. In another situation, she may be the counsellor for both a woman who feels betrayed and permanently wounded by her husband's affair and for a husband who feels beaten down and humiliated by his wife's seemingly inexhaustible rage. *Developing the art of this kind of counselling is the recurrent theme of this book and, I hope, of each relational counsellor's lifelong thinking.* Multi-directional partiality is an achievement of attitude more than of technique. The relational counsellor learns to think: 'What happened to each and all these people?' rather than: 'What are these people doing to this one person?' Multi-directional partiality may be a way of being which is particularly nourished by the person-centred approach. Talking about breakdowns in communication, Carl Rogers has written:

> This tendency to react to any emotionally meaningful statement by forming an evaluation of it from our own point of view is . . . the major barrier to interpersonal communication. . . . Real communication occurs and this evaluative tendency is avoided when we listen with understanding. It means to see the expressed idea and attitude from the other person's point of view, to sense how it feels to him, to achieve his frame of reference in regard to the thing he is talking about. (Rogers, 1961b: 331–2)

Box 1.1 Listening to multiple realities

In the following example, the counsellors attempt to fully understand all sides in a complex developmental dispute. As is typical in relational counselling as it will be described in this book, the counsellors also make efforts to create a structure in which a dialogue can take place.

Two parents, Beverly and Hal, consulted a counsellor about a severe rift with their 22-year-old son, Alex. Dependent on them for financial support and now in his fifth, and presumably last, year of undergraduate work at a university, Alex has withdrawn from the pre-medical school course in which he had been doing well to begin taking courses in elementary education preparatory to getting a teaching certificate. His parents are hurt, angry, frustrated and baffled. It was not for this that they invested thousands of dollars in the cost of private preparatory school and the full cost of education at one of the country's most prestigious and expensive universities.

They cut off support, forcing Alex to take out loans to continue his education as well as having to work to support himself. There was continued sporadic contact by phone characterized by rejecting angry words on both sides – then missed phone calls on both sides on family occasions.

In my meetings with the parents, they described a young man who was totally self-absorbed, impulsive, rebelling for the sake of rebelling and only interested in his parents for their money. They felt they were in a battle to avoid paying for him to indulge his 'lazy, incompetent avoidance of the use of his real talents!' They also revealed their suffering from a drastic change in their relationship with Hal's father. 'We're getting it from all generations!' Hal's father, a successful professional, was gradually withdrawing because of slowly worsening Alzheimer's disease. Hal was mourning the loss of his father's presence, vitality and interest. He had been used to sharp, involved contact with his father and now he was dealing with what seemed to be an 'empty shell'. The emotional cut-off with his son – brief angry contacts or superficial avoiding contacts –

paralleled the way that age and disease were cutting off contact with his father.

What did *not* take place in our meetings was any attempt to tell the parents that they had no right to tell their grown son what to study. The counsellor did not take it on himself additionally to judge them for their desire to control by means of their money. They were honest and blunt: '*Of course* the money had strings attached!' And they, like most other clients, did not come to counselling because they lacked the intelligence to grasp conventional respect for autonomous choice. The more they talked, the more complex the picture became. They admitted that Alex had many qualities such as hard work and good will, as shown by his gentle involvement with the older members of their extended family. They also felt he was impulsive, easily led (by others) and, it seemed to them, possibly influenced to make a radical career change because of a young woman he was seeing.

When, after much ambivalence was expressed on both sides, Alex came 'home' to visit, parents and son agreed to have a family meeting with the parents' counsellor.

The counsellor suggested that he invite a female counsellor who did not know the parents. He asked that the parents and young man agree that the meeting would not include threatening to disown each other or refusing to speak if the other didn't do their will. (They could do that on their own without the expense and trouble of counselling!) He sought agreement in advance to two sessions with a day or more in between. It is expected in such meetings that the first session will often include accusation and the opening up of issues. Commitment to come for a second session allows for overnight healing and for more accepting and flexible attitudes to emerge. In general, the counsellor was asking a kind of commitment and preparation that is particularly helpful in intergenerational meetings in which emotions are expected to be strong and impulse may lead conversation to be prematurely cut off (Framo, 1992).

The sessions themselves surprised all participants, including the counsellors, who had prepared a second office in which to talk separately with both parties if the room couldn't hold the heat of the discussion. Beverly and Hal came prepared to listen as well as speak. They had really not spoken to Alex in a year. He was older and had been through some hard times and had learned from them. Undefensive, he agreed with all of their arguments about the cost and potential foolishness of what he was doing. He talked at length about how little he had made his own decisions about his future, but did not describe this as his parents' fault but as a habit it was now his task to outgrow. The meeting included his lively narrative of what his year had been like – his first year ever of self-support. He got a grasp of what his parents' year had been like – their first ever in which they were left in the dark about their son's thinking process. Phone calls and missed phone calls were explained. A lot of time and some tears were spent talking about the boy's grandfather and the plight of his father in being without his two closest male family members and friends.

In the middle of all this mutual understanding and empathy there were still lots of accusations, lots of raised voices, lots of briefly attempted ultimatums, which in the end were only temporary expressions of feeling one's own back to the wall. The counsellors facilitated each person's fair chance to be heard and trusted that the outcome would be positive without having an agenda that anyone change his or her perspective. The family was amused as well as pleased by the existence of a second room. 'We won't need it', they said casually, and they were right. The voiceless boy within the son was merged with the voice and social skill of the young adult. The parents' introjected images of frustrated attempts to be heard by other family members living and dead surfaced but did not dominate. They were in the presence of their son who was just himself, not a father or mother or brother from the past. Persons experienced in the person-centred approach may be reminded of a truth almost inevitably attained at the end of every successful encounter group: '*I didn't know that about you*'.

Alex continued to study for a field that interested him more than medicine. His parents continued to disapprove, but as people with strong opinions, rather than outraged guardians. He acknowledged that he did not have a right to their financial support for his decisions. They acknowledged that they can love a son who chooses a life that is different from their intentions.

Creating person-centred relational counselling

At this time there is no person-centred family counselling which exists as a set of techniques in its own right (see also Gaylin, 1989: 275). A counsellor who has worked to absorb the best of the person-centred approach should work in a way that is responsive to each family she meets. For a beginning discussion, however, I offer the model that I derive from rereading Rogers' presentation (1959) of the core principles of what was then called Client Centred Therapy. This model gives a meaningful way of looking at the counsellor's tasks as well as those of the client. Each person-centred counsellor may have a bedrock of principles such as those highlighted below. For me, person-centred relational counselling is a dialogue between these principles and the challenges of facilitating a conversation among intimates. Here, in italics, is the model, as I see it. Each assertion is followed by reflections relevant to relational counselling.

One person seeks to become aware of, to symbolize accurately and to accept all parts of herself. This is the congruent person; the facilitator, the counsellor, a person highly committed to work on herself. She brings that commitment to work on self into the presence of a couple or family.

As a relational counsellor, I need supervision to help me identify the urgent likes and dislikes, hopes and fears that arise in me when I meet my clients. Helpfulness derives from my awareness of where I end and where my clients begin. Chapter 5, Preparation for Relational Therapy, describes my own efforts at awareness of myself in relation to my work.

The relational counsellor trusts that his self-aware presence will be useful for a family. He must engage with them – observing, noticing reactions and needs so that he may facilitate their entering the counselling process. He will also have to do whatever it takes – moving around, making coffee, breathing deeply, opening windows – to keep from being swept away from his own centre. For example, with an angry couple he may need to say: 'Wait. Give me a minute to slow down here and catch my breath. Let me tell you what I've got so far!' rather than sink into his chair as though listening to his own parents argue.

There is less and less difference between her concept of herself and what she thinks she should be; therefore, she has less and less she has to defend against. Carl Rogers describes the incongruence of one person as the heart of the process of a deteriorating relationship and the *presence of a congruent person* as the key to an improving relationship. The person-centred counsellor seeks to be the one who is least defensive. In relation to family and couples work, she does not have to be defensive of herself as expert, as someone who knows the answers; she does not have to be defensive of a theory that she is applying to the clients' situation; she does not have to be defensive because she is insistent on her agenda as the only path to change; she does not have to be defensive because she is on the side of one person against another. She is a 'non-anxious presence' to use the words of family therapist Edgar Friedman (1991: 138).

The family counsellor must notice if some unruly personal expectation walked into the room with his clients, for example: 'You had better have an answer for what to do with this sullen 14-year-old'; or 'This is our last session and I don't have anything to say that will wrap it all up for them'; or 'These folks need a counsellor! Not me!'

And therefore she has the freedom to see and hear another person actively and objectively. Without an agenda she has nothing better to do than to seek to understand each person's point of view. Her clients may say of her that, more than other counsellors they had seen, she seemed to listen to them and to be interested in what they thought was important. Carl Rogers (1980) cited disturbing research indicating a decrease in counsellor empathy with greater experience in the field! The family counsellor's ability to make listening a priority is the centerpiece of a recent study on work with so-called impossible cases. (Duncan et al., 1997a).

The freedom to hear is blocked by many obstacles in couples counselling in particular. Bernard Guerney (1998) talks about the *empathizer* and the *expressor* role in important relationships: that you can't be both at the same time! For example, I cannot hear very well when I am focused on the predetermined lessons my clients need to be taught (see Chapter 9 for discussion of this dynamic).

And she is more able to receive people as they are with regard that is less and less conditional because of her expectations. She will be less pressured, less anxious. She will not feel called upon to impose expectations on her clients. She will enjoy them and herself more. This returning attention to the client has been a consistent theme of all supervision I have offered or received. Letting go of expectations is the road away from aligning yourself with one client against another. Family therapist Molly Layton writes: 'To tune into the client, I have to let go of my own demand to fix or understand them. I might have to abandon my hard-won sense of knowing, my prized experience and instead sit there, open, expectant, empty' (1995).

Family members are frequently burdened with expectations from the wider society, in addition to those they impose on one another. The counsellor may quickly (though subtly) introject those same expectations so that, without knowing it, he has just joined the 'Oh, just go to school!' team for a child or the 'Just close your eyes and think of England!' school of thought for a partner who has lost interest in sex. It may be even more of a struggle for a counsellor to accept clients who impose strong expectations on one another: 'Why can't you just leave him alone!'

Another person is able to experience that his communication is received without judgement. Clients will feel less pressured and less anxious. They will be less likely to perceive the difficulties of relationship as the result of their own inadequacy. The literature of family therapy is filled with emphasis on the positive (Hoffman, 1998: 154). Not judging is a condition for the positive being discovered. Elsewhere, Rogers has described the 'evaluative tendency' as the primary barrier to good interpersonal relationships (Rogers, 1961b: 331–2).

In a recent presentation, a leading writer about families in relation to schools, courts, churches and social service agencies emphasized the many ways parents feel judged, disliked and dismissed by those who see themselves as advocates for children (Taffel, 1998). A systems perspective (see Chapter 3) would indicate the impossibility of helping children whose parents feel despised and demeaned.

And that person feels the increasing possibility of being understood. Clients may be more likely to share of the truest parts of themselves when a counsellor or other family members show understanding. Information and creativity that was formerly withheld can be shared. The clients may speak less out of role or their image of what they should be and share something closer to who they are. It is exciting to watch the effect on a father when he realizes the counsellor is interested in what he really thinks; or the clarity that becomes possible when a teenager is talking less to prove or defend himself than to say what is truly on his mind.

Rogers' emphasis on the tentative respectful nature of empathic listening in individual counselling (1980) is mirrored by the family counsellor's careful efforts to find out if her perception is accurate. Two contemporary family therapists have written: 'The therapist never understands, but is always in the process of understanding better' (Goolishian and Anderson, 1992). In couples counselling, each member of a couple may feel great relief when he or she feels empathic attention to their individual situation *and* the predicament each shares with their partner. Couples may say, 'No wonder we can't talk to each other!'

And feels positive regard that he experiences as unconditional. Members of a couple or family can feel the counsellor's acceptance of them individually and as a group. A family member can feel valued without feeling disloyal or unfair because the counsellor accepts her companions as well as her.

Family counsellors often study their own relationships with their family of origin. They can sometimes understand from the inside out why a father would withhold love or attention or why a mother would develop a habit of chronic criticism. They may have new insight into why children don't do their chores and why sisters can quarrel bitterly. They may learn the way a family can adapt well to one child and be often anxious around another. Ivan Boszormenyi-Nagy et al. (1991) define a process called *exoneration*, in which, without denying the reality of any injury, a person may come to understand the predicament of those who injured him. This personal exploration allows the counsellor to truly accept clients rather than merely portray acceptance of them.

Therefore they become increasingly able to become aware of, symbolize accurately and accept all parts of themselves, including those which have been previously rejected. Clients become congruent. Instead of making one another's faults or defects the object of their attention, they become more familiar with and accepting of their own ways of being. They project less; are less pessimistic; are more objective. One client described the couples counselling of her and her husband as 'the one place where we can talk. It is where I can be myself and feel that I am seeing what's real for him.' The couples counsellor offers a consistent acceptance and realness which encourages the risk of the truth. Defensive or accusatory language can give way to more 'softening' words (Koerner and Jacobson, 1994: 219) which allow greater objectivity. For example, saying 'I was disappointed,' rather than 'You are the most self-centred person I have ever met.'

There is less difference between clients' concepts of self and what they think they should be. Clients are released from the pressure of 'conditions of worth' and are at home with themselves and with each other. They carry less baggage from their family of origins. They are less mystified and anxious.

In some of the family of origin therapies, such as that of Murray Bowen, clients look at their growing-up family situation through a genogram or family map. Sometimes the simple act of seeing one's family placement can give insight into the expectations one carries and the habitual sense of not measuring up which can infuse interpersonal relations.

They have less need for defensiveness. This most sought-after condition is the state in which intimates can communicate without confusion about what things are really like. Problems are cut down to size; people know where they stand; communication is more interesting and becomes more an unfolding than a dreary repetition.

American researcher John Gottman (1994) has described defensiveness as one of the 'Four Horsemen of the Apocalypse' whose persistent presence in a relationship predicts divorce.

They become more and more able to see and hear one another actively and objectively. Family members can become less directed by anxiety-driven distortions of communication. Actions can be undertaken for their own sake rather than as covert ways to influence others. Children can become themselves rather than projections of their parents. Couples can see one another clearly rather than live out battles based on introjected ideas about what males and females are supposed to be and do.

Murray Bowen (Friedman, 1991) has described the 'undifferentiated ego mass' in which people are driven by emotional reactions triggered by other family members rather than by their own integrated responses. His approach offers ways in which encounters with members of one's family of origin can free a person from endless doomed efforts to impress, protect, convert, correct or otherwise control or be controlled by significant others.

How does a counsellor steeped in a person-centred model of personal growth and congruence make the transition from individual to family and couples work? The next chapter will respond to common questions about counsellor perspective and Chapter 3 will present common themes of work with families and couples.

CHAPTER 2

Why Do Counsellors Stay Away from Relational Counselling?

Sigmund Freud blocked the door to family consultation for his lifetime and a decade after, leaving 'a conviction that it was counter-productive and dangerous for a therapist to become involved with more than one member of the same family' (Broderick and Schrader, 1991: 19). Carl Rogers, while going against the analytic trend of his times in so many other ways, developed a way of working with individuals that focused on the value of the here and now presence and relationship of a single counsellor and a single client.

Many counsellors, having experienced the dramatic events that take place in individual therapy, may wonder how, in a family or couples session, they would convey the same respect, attention to personal unfolding and patient expectation of the actualizing tendency at work. What are the changes in perspective and positive experiences which lead counsellors to feel they can be their effective selves while seeing a couple or family? In this chapter I will explore responses to the most common concerns that hold counsellors back from embarking upon relational counselling.

Fear that the tasks of the family counsellor will be inconsistent with a person-centred background

At the heart of the person-centred approach, applied in individual counselling, is the persistent expectation that, given certain conditions, a person can flourish in a way which is more rich and lasting than a therapist could predict or direct. Effective relational counsellors use different language, but rely on the same phenomenon. 'I don't always know exactly where we are going, but I know we are going somewhere,' family therapist Virginia Satir once told her clients (Satir, 1972). Relational counsellors develop the expectation that there are *overlooked* attempts at order, effectiveness and connection in the most chaotic, discouraged and unloving relationships. They have a stubborn expectation that there is an *'alternate story'* to the *'problem saturated stories'* (White and Epston, 1990: 16, my emphasis) with which clients can present. I believe this relates closely to what Carl Rogers described as the *'formative directional tendency'*:

> [it is] an evolutionary tendency toward greater order, greater complexity, greater interrelatedness. In humankind, this tendency exhibits itself as the individual moves from a single cell origin to complex organic functioning, to knowing and sensing below the level of consciousness, to a conscious awareness of the organism and the external world, to a transcendent awareness of the harmony and unity of the cosmic system, including humankind. (Rogers, 1980: 133)

Several relational counsellors I interviewed while researching this book described their own image of the *formative directional tendency* in their work, although few of them had studied Rogers enough to know the concept. One colleague, Breffni Barrett, said: 'The time I really notice this is when I am doing co-therapy with a less experienced counsellor. Before and after session, they keep saying things like "These parents don't have a clue about how to deal with these kids" or "This marriage doesn't have a chance" while I think "Let's wait a while – let's see what this family comes up with."'

Family therapist David Sanders has provided me with an example of the formative directional tendency particularly activated by the medium of relational counselling. David was appointed family therapist for a large family who were being seen individually by at least five therapists. One of them, a psychiatrist, was convinced that the only way to save the life of his patient (the mother of the family) was an extended hospitalization. The family therapist, asked only to facilitate a family meeting to prepare for the mother's hospitalization, found instead that the clients had become empowered to discuss alternatives to the mother's hospitalization. Everyone, including the very depressed, formerly suicidal mother, became active in fighting to avoid this treatment which, while logical for the mother's individual health, would have been demoralizing to the family. As individual client, the mother was only a distressed person in great need; in relation to her family she was able also to be a reliable and responsive person.

Another family therapist, Eliot Weinstein, told me:

> Here's an example of why I work with families. I was seeing an individual. He presented as a supreme victim and underdog. His persistent story was how incompetent he was to deal with the world's challenges. Even his clothes were wrong! They seemed just picked up off the floor at random. He had scattered thoughts and loose associations. In frustration, I asked him to invite his family in. When they came in I was struck by an amazing difference. He attended to his kids and attended to his wife. He presented as sure in his roles. The transformation was amazing. I look for a medium

that enhances the best: the stance that allows individuals to present with strong colours. Family therapy brings out the best part of a person. They are no longer fragmented.

The case example in Box 2.1 may serve to illustrate the way family counselling can turn from awkward conversation to the formation of a self-directing process in which the whole family offers a more meaningful and durable healing than any one member could achieve or than the counsellor could predict.

Box 2.1 The formative tendency emerges

I was the family counsellor for two reserved older parents and their two children who were in their late teens. They were referred to a clinic because their oldest son Fred, 18, quiet and somewhat isolated socially, had been caught in his first criminal offence, using an illegal drug. The prospect of family counselling was, at first, very bleak for them. What could they do except talk in discouraged tones about their silent and shamed Fred while bringing their successful gregarious younger son Michael, 17, for inconvenient discussion of a problem that seemed to have nothing to do with him?

Indeed, at first, the family meetings focused inevitably on the seemingly simple disgrace of the older boy and the frustration of the family about the drug matter, along with several other disappointing aspects of his life. Well backed in supervision by a supportive team, the counsellor persisted in broadening the discussion to the life of the family. Many other facts emerged, the most prominent of which was that the father was dying of an inoperable cancer. Also revealed was a family business at a crucial point, partly affected by the father's decline. The family managed to remember Fred's many non-academic, non-athletic talents, including hard, reliable work since he was a little boy. Fred was made less isolated by the recognition that his shyness was shared by his father. The family remembered the long love story between the parents which included the triumph over an earlier illness of the father's. In general they began to ackowledge Fred's quieter abilities as well as his brother Michael's impressive social and academic success.

The counselling attended to many aspects of family life, including: response to evaluation of Fred's potential drug problem; the family's adjustment to *both* teenagers becoming adults; and a playful intervention in which a whole session was spent defining and attempting to correct *Michael's* faults. (The counsellor asked him to spend the session in the chair of the 'kid in trouble'. This provoked some hilarity, much relief for Fred and some serious exploration of worries about Michael who was fairly constantly in the position of one who, 'always OK', was rarely seen in his vulnerable side.) The last two sessions of the therapy were spent in moving exploration of the father's feelings about leaving his family. He told Fred he needed his help and made several specific requests to the son to take care of certain aspects of the business. Fred agreed to the additional help requested and indeed had already been showing himself to be helpful. Everyone was tearful including the therapist. The last interaction of the counselling was a letter to the family at the time of the father's death.

In this example it seemed initially unpromising to work with a family in which roles were clearly and rigidly distributed. It felt uncomfortable and rude of the counsellor to suggest family work (although it was the policy of the agency at that time) and it seemed easier just to see the son who was required to see someone. The counsellor proceeded because of the expectation that family counselling would highlight resources which would be hidden or stagnant if individual counselling was the only medium. The counselling described above followed a pattern common in family therapy. Initial awkwardness, rigidity and fear that we are wasting time, leading to a search for common ground in which a new view of both problems and resources is expanded. Eventually, the therapy focused away from its initial purpose around a crisis of one member and into an area defined by the whole family as most meaningful.

Fear I will not be competent to see more than one person at once

Speaking, as he often did, like a Zen Master, the late family therapist Carl Whitaker used to refer to 'the weapon of my own impotence' (Simon, 1985). A common predicament for family members is the expectation that they have power in an area in which they in fact have none – like making a teenager listen *carefully* to a lecture! They increase their distress by failing to use the power that they do have – like finding a way to spend time with a teenager, on *his* terms. The counsellor is competent because she knows in what ways she is *not* in control and is free from distracting efforts to prove her importance or defend any position. She *does* have power over herself: the power of extending herself through interest and attention; the power to notice behaviours other than those of the family's 'problem saturated story' (White and Epston, 1990). Without holding an agenda, she has the power of speaking clearly with her own voice and owning her reactions rather than speaking strategically, hoping to have an effect by her cleverness. Most important, she can channel her strength and ingenuity toward the facilitation of each person's ability to know and express his point of view and to tolerate similar expression by his partner or family members.

In family and couples work, description of what you are doing can bring confidence to counsellor and clients alike. In the following phrases, the counsellor is explaining his role in the process as well as sharing some of the values that underlie his work:

> *In a session in which children are joining the ongoing counselling of their parents*: I wanted to meet all of you at once because I'm sure everyone has an opinion about dad and mom's plan to separate, but I don't think everyone has had a chance to say it.

> *In a second session*: The main method I have to offer is that Joyce would have a chance to say all that she wants heard on the subject while Bob and I listen, trying to understand and knowing that we don't have to agree. We then can find out if we have listened well by saying what we have understood without trying to rebut or judge. Then it will be Bob's turn, with Joyce and me listening and trying to understand without having to agree.

> *In a first session*: Right after a divorce, everyone asks how do you feel about it and kids always say 'OK' or 'I don't know'. I want to ask two questions: 'What was it like then, now that you can look back on it? And what is it like now?'

> *In the middle of a fifth session with a family of two parents and two teenagers*: Are we on the right topic? Mary, I think you are signalling that there is something else we might be talking about.

The counsellor feels competent because she knows how useful congruent meetings can be for relationships in distress. Person-centred counsellor Maureen O'Hara described her sources of confidence in meeting with couples and families as follows: 'I trust people. I trust conversation will find a way through. It is also because I don't have specific outcomes in mind as we begin.' The counsellor is competent because she respects the possibilities of the meeting: people being informed; people being understood; people correcting misunderstandings; people finding common ground. Remembering the difference it makes when people even partially understand each other at an important moment or about an important issue increases the value I attach to even awkward, difficult family meetings. Because of the harm done by mistaken impressions acted on as though they were fact, the work of patient facilitation seems invaluable. My competence derives from my faithfulness to this basic but essential task.

Fear that one or more people will become angry and the session will end in an unsatisfying way

People *do* get angry in relational counselling. Anger can be frightening or difficult to deal with, but under favourable conditions, its expression can lead to a significant shift in a relationship. Anger can bring life to a relationship because of its ability to generate heat and overcome the restricting influence of excessive rationality. Anger can act as a motivator in its ability to highlight dissonance in a way that dispassionate reflection could let go for years. Finally, anger expressed without rejection can be a form of commitment. Anger brings chaos into the relationship and with chaos comes the possibility of reorganization at a higher level.

Anger has another side, however. Anger can become a habit – a fixed, unimaginative way of relating which, instead of leading to new connection, leaves one or more members of the family stuck in dreary, choreographed recitals of injuries or subject to frightening outbursts of rage. One person with anger as habit is generally accompanied by a person who is withdrawn, passive-aggressive and acting out in some secret way, for example, by an affair. Two people with anger as habit are each lonely inside a circle of accusation and defence.

The counsellor's presence matters in the expression of anger. He puts it in context, punctuates it and makes sense out of it. It is not just anger expressed, but anger which is expressed in a counsellor's office. This does not mean anger denied, forbidden or turned by clever wordplay into something more positive, and thus misunderstood. The counsellor dialogues with the angry person as well as with that person's partner. He sometimes may direct his attention away from the angry person and toward another family member in a request for a comment on the anger. It is anger met rather than poured out in monologue.

The counsellor may ask what is the meaning of this anger, expressed here in this office in the presence of someone who is not a family member? All are encouraged to participate in answering this question. The counsellor models freedom not to accept anger as a given, but as a roadmap to learning and connection. In family therapy, *terminal language*, or defining people as static nouns, gives way to *process language* which describes action and felt reactions (Falicov, 1986). Without taking away a person's right to his feelings, the counsellor exerts a right to be heard, a right to respond and a right not to have to pretend that the only person present is the angry one.

Fear of stirring things up between people in a harmful way

Families are already stirred up when they come to see a counsellor. Rogers' second core condition is an important one: the client(s) are in a state of incongruence. Without trouble, counselling can be unfocused (and awkward and stilted, as I experienced with one cheery couple and one contented family who tried conjoint therapy just because they thought it would be an interesting experience!).

Breffni Barrett tells of a family in which the parents were reluctant to bring in the children who were 10 and 12 because they didn't want them exposed to their parents' problems. When the children were present, they were asked if they knew their parents often disagreed and were very angry with each other. The parents were surprised to find their children to be highly articulate about several fights they had overheard, tensions they had noticed and habitual disagreements they took for granted. It is usually an illusion for couples to think that their estrangement is kept secret from their children no matter how good they are at lowering their voices.

Does the family act out more because of having come for counselling? It is my experience that families come in when life at home is so troubled by unwanted events and feelings that relief is sought. The family will act out some of their chaos by way of introduction in the counselling sessions. A family member may sense an oncoming explosion and bring the family for counselling in an attempt to head it off. The negative effect expressed, clarified and contained in their family counselling session may prevent a child running away from home, a marital separation, physical violence or depression.

Fear of real or perceived alignment with one or more members of the family against other members

The concept of multi-directional partiality (see Chapter 1) encourages counsellor alliance with each family and couple member. The counsellor is on the side of each person. She understands, cares about, has compassion for and hopes for each person's growth and liberation. Effective relational counselling means a commitment to transcend our prejudices not because of some great virtue, but because the assumption that *anyone* is less deserving of understanding inevitably blocks progress. The relational counsellor reminds herself frequently that people co-create their interactions.

Because it is so easy to align with one individual, some counsellors will not do family or couples therapy without a co-therapist. Maureen O'Hara, James Framo and others have expressed the conviction that two people of different genders are needed so that the family is not victimized by the counsellor's over-identification with his own gender or the clients' perception that this would be so. In an interview Maureen O'Hara said, 'I don't want a man to feel as though he is being ganged up on by two women'. The two counsellors can offer different types of empathy for each member of the family. Each person perceives an ally who knows particularly what it's like for her or him while feeling safe in the knowledge that everyone is represented.

Other therapists are less concerned about gender, but simply maintain that two people are needed. Carl Whitaker (Whitaker and Keith, 1981) always encouraged co-therapy so that one therapist could express a spontaneous 'crazy' side that in acting out – stirring things up, saying unacceptable things and bringing up threatening topics – would add a needed emotional balance to the family encounter. This is possible because there is another therapist who is able to be the grown-up looking out for everyone's safety, boundaries, hurts and needs.

My own approach is to see families without another counsellor, but to consult frequently with counsellors of both genders. One reason for this is economic – most agencies and clients are not able to afford two therapists at once. The notion that relational counselling would take an extreme amount of effort and would involve the careful scheduling of multiple counsellors is one reason why it is not practised as frequently as its helpfulness would warrant.

Alignment is best dealt with by the counsellor's openness and encouragement of client sharing of any discomfort or perceived judgement or unfairness. It is this author's contention that counsellors align all the time – often in ways related to gender, but not necessarily in favour of one's own gender. Frequent frank supervision is invaluable for catching unspoken bias in action. A supervisor may ask: 'What was the purpose of that statement or question?' If my purpose was somehow to be a representative of one client to another – to protect or to teach a lesson – I can, without defensiveness, begin to own my role and express my concerns or intentions more directly.

Fear that having grown up in an unhappy family myself, I will be unable to relate to a family in a positive way

Many counsellors describe their early experiences in family life as difficult and negative. Whether this is because their expectations of family life are very high or because they were drawn to the field to resolve their greater than usual problems I cannot say. Virginia Satir used to say that since she noticed so many secrets and unexplained troubles in her own family, she resolved at a young age to become 'a family detective'. I once asked a group of 20 counsellors in training how many of them felt that they could have talked in a real way to their parents when they were teenagers. One person raised her hand. It is wise for counsellors to be aware of the limits of their family experiences and not to project them onto others either by assuming the worst or trying to impose the best on the very diverse families they meet. Further, in family just as in individual counselling, the work of supervision and training is to learn to respect our own feelings and reactions and to distinguish them from those of our clients.

One of my colleagues, Ron Urone, was attracted to family therapy because of the sense of empowerment he got by writing a family biography for a graduate course. In this exercise which involved describing his family on paper, he was able to discover a sense of self that was very different from the role he felt placed in or the family myths that described him. Because of that, he said, 'I was able to have some key conversations with my mother. I was able to tell her how I felt crazy around her and why and what I wanted to do about it.' This excellent counsellor, in touch with much suffering in his own family, became aware of how empowered people can become to have even awkward conversations with significant others. Good experience of personal work on your family of origin can give personal experience of the formative tendency at work. Box 2.2 describes the fortunate circumstance under which Carl Rogers managed the often difficult task of differentiating from one's family of origin while staying connected with them.

Box 2.2   Carl Rogers and his family of origin

There are many references throughout his extensive writings that show Carl Rogers' connection with the themes that family therapists describe and encounter. Most remarkable, perhaps, are his own autobiographical descriptions of his change in relation to his own family of origin. Recalling a six-month trip to China during his junior year in college he comments:

This voyage bears curious testimony to the fact that speed of communication is not always desirable. During the trip I kept a long typed journal of the various events I was living through and my reactions to them. . . . I sent a copy of this journal to Helen who was now definitely my sweetheart and another copy to my family. Since we did not have the benefit of airmail it took two months for a reply to arrive. *Thus I kept pouring out on paper all my new feelings and ideas and thoughts with no notion of the consternation that this was causing in my family. By the time their reactions caught up with me, the rift in outlook was fully established* [italics mine]. Thus, with a minimum of pain I broke the intellectual and religious ties with my home . . .

Due to this six months trip I had been able freely, and with no sense of defiance or guilt, to think my own thoughts, come to my own conclusions and to take the stands I believe in. This process had achieved a real direction and assurance – which never after wavered – before I had any inkling that it constituted rebellion from home. From the date of this trip, my goals, values, aims and philosophy have been my own and very divergent from the views which my parents held and which I had held up to this point. Psychologically, it was a most important period of declaring my independence from my family. (Rogers, 1967)

Rogers describes a process that happened to him in a natural way. He communicated who he was and shared openly with his family and loved ones without getting entangled either in defiance or conformity – the goal of much family therapeutic work. His personal account also shows the paradox and idiosyncrasy that often accompanies family change. He got to share what was on his mind, but was blessedly exempt from having to hear an immediate answer! He could finish what he had to say to his parents without rebuttal – an event many people long for. Not his usual idea of good communication, but one that for that transition was just right.

Fear of being overwhelmed by all the data in a multi-person meeting

Counsellors who are afraid they cannot gather or organize all the data coming in are accurate in their fear. No family member ever has the entire answer – and neither does any counsellor. An overload of data is the rule and not the exception. More is happening than can be commented upon, much less resolved to everyone's satisfaction. There are as many events taking place as there are people present in the room. Six people will have six different stories about the counselling hour. Furthermore, each of those stories will change in relation to further interactions and reflections outside the hour.

Family therapist Peggy Papp has written:

> One trainee [at the Ackerman Institute's Depression in Context Project] asked me how, as therapists, we could possibly keep track of so many elements in therapy – all that, plus clients' work situations, biological predisposition, multi-generational family histories, distressing life events and more. My answer to her was that *we would have to let the families lead us*. Learning to listen to the system and determine the multiple influences on the depressed client has been the mainstay of our method and provides us with many more therapeutic options. (Papp, 1996: 54–5)

My own sense of confidence in family and couples work comes from my acceptance of the limits of my control. In knowing that the counsellor will *never* have enough data to be sure of an expert intervention, I am allowed the human path of sharing my hearing of concerns, contradictions and understanding of the burdens experienced by the family. I give myself permission not to know how an impasse will be resolved, as well as to know that impasses do get resolved when there is listening, self-disclosure and attention to new feelings which emerge only in the conversation.

The counsellor can never take in or manage enough data to singlehandedly solve family problems. His job lies in another direction. He is there to empower each individual in the family to gather data well enough for them to be able to proceed in a constructive direction. In my experience as a client in counselling with my own family, I invariably found the (very competent) counsellor always slightly off the mark, never entirely accurate in any attempt made to categorize my experience. But many doors were opened by her listening as best she could, by her questions, and by the very fact that she had a vision of the father or husband (me!) that was different than my own – as do my wife and children! The idea that she had a different slant on family information gave me the gift not of her perspective but of knowing that another perspective is possible.

A frequent family expectation is: 'I ought to have enough data to be able to change this or that other family member.' As Virginia Satir (1972) said to a family member in a videotaped session, 'I'm getting the feeling that there is a rule that you are supposed to know what to do in this family.' The counsellor models not having enough data and never being able to gather enough data in order to help or handle someone else's problems. The counsellor also models being able to trust one's own ability to gather certain data: like what one feels right now; what one's fundamental intention is or was; what one wants; what one is most worried about; what one would do if one didn't feel responsible for acting perfectly.

CHAPTER 3

Themes in Family Therapy

Every established school of relational therapy may be seen as attempting to respond to some valid need which arises in relationship living. The most resourceful person in the room is a client and the best assistant is the counsellor who has hope, good will, curiosity and commitment. *How* to be present in such a way that resources are highlighted is a question that in family counselling has as many answers as there are therapists. The themes of family counselling, described below, may be seen as a way of responding to what families bring when they come into counselling.

In this exploration of family counselling and the person-centred approach, I intend to be reflective about each approach rather than defensive. Each aspect of relationship therapy contains *a large idea* – an important organizing concept whose reality may be acknowledged even while the consequent therapeutic approach may be challenged. All the following approaches have been responsive to the needs of thousands of families and have been taught to most persons about to practice family therapy.

In this chapter, I will discuss five interrelated concepts about *systems thinking* held by most relational counsellors, as well the systems aspects of Carl Rogers' work. I will then describe concepts, familiar to relational counsellors, which offer a clear picture of issues in a human system. Finally I will present three characteristics of relational counsellor behaviours that are shared among the different approaches: couples and family counsellors are generally *active*; they often *reframe*; they often *ask questions*.

Systems thinking

The relational counsellor thinks of a family or any social grouping as a living system. Drawing on many concepts from the physical sciences and the study of biological and organizational systems, the family and couples counsellor lives with ideas such as the following:

The whole is greater than the sum of its parts. This concept informs the counsellor to strive for a wide lens understanding of a family or couple's life rather than to focus on a single unit within a system. For example, in a family in which one member has symptoms of depression, the family as a whole may be seen as undergoing difficulty, one sign of which is a member's depression. Without denying the reality of the individual's experience, the conversation can be expanded to a discussion of all the difficulties faced by the entire family group. From this perspective the symptom can be a kind of language which leads to awareness of all the pressures, internal and external, which result in only one observable symptom.

Therefore any change in one part of a system affects the whole system. Family counselling derives much hopefulness from this concept. A family can be seen as stuck because its members are repetitively trying to solve a problem by focusing on a single part of the system in which, for whatever reason, they are blocked. A systems perspective may give freedom to seek leverage in another area. For example, a family organized around a pattern of constant punishment for a teenager's poor schoolwork performance, may, in conversation, be reminded that the decline in schoolwork coincided with a grandparent's illness and a parent's preoccupation away from many nurturing, pleasant activities with that teenager. From this perspective, the systems information gives a family a wider range of options for seeking change.

Therefore causality is not linear, but circular. The systems thinker is less likely to ascribe values such as good and bad or right and wrong when a family drama is unfolding. For example, the notion that a father criticizes because his daughter underachieves or that daughter underachieves because her father criticizes can give way to the notion that both are in a cycle expressive of a whole system meeting the complex demands of a young member approaching adulthood. The systems-thinking therapist does not think of straightening out a father who is victimizing a daughter; and thinks even less of joining the father in urging the daughter to work harder. She is more likely to join the two in exploring dimensions of other events and perceptions that landed them in this fix.

Therefore there is no identified patient to be cured in the midst of an otherwise healthy system. In other language, there is *no scapegoat* on which a family can focus to change generalized anxiety into a focused, though frustrating, problem. In this concept lies the consistent belief in human flexibility and resiliency, and avoidance of pathologizing, which makes relational counselling compatible with the person-centred approach. The individual is seen as neither intrinsically possessing disease or deficit conditions nor stuck with a permanent tendency to live out symptoms. Instead individual reality is seen as co-created and resolvable as a family or couple becomes freed to enjoy a wider variety of perceptions and behaviours. Systems thinking, like the person-centred approach, leads to the view that people are always in process, always complex. For example there is no purely 'dependent' person, except in the presence of someone who is 'codependent' within a system that exerts control on both to stay in those roles.

Therefore the process of therapy may be seen as uncovering, bypassing, or redefining implicit rules not only of behaviour, but also of perception. The relational counsellor becomes accustomed to the way families repeat sequences of behaviour. There is a story that, in the early days of videotaping family meetings, a cameraman was noticed to have an uncanny ability to direct the camera to wherever the next action or speech was about to occur. When asked about one particular camera movement he replied, 'Oh, I know that whenever mother speaks, Johnny will follow up with a comment. So I always turn the camera toward him when she finishes!' Family members also seem to repeat patterns of thinking. For example, a common couples' dilemma is the way one person will withhold information about an area of life, such as his office, while the other feels alternately suspicious and excluded. One member of a couple needs only to mention the words 'office staff' for the other to become angry, critical and inquisitorial. Her partner is drawn to withholding inconsequential information about office staff just as one might find a strange attraction to touch the third rail in an underground station! A relational counsellor is able to be effective sometimes by noticing and commenting on a deviation in the pattern that those within it may not notice.

To expand the systems approach even more, some authors discuss a systemic relationship between the many parts of the self within the individual, which must be reconciled along with the many selves in the external family (Schwarz, 1987). Within the person-centred approach, Mearns (1999) talks about a 'family of configurations within the self'; and from a humanistic integrative approach, Rowan (1990) refers to 'subpersonalities'. Following Salvador Minuchin (1974), many therapists describe subsystems – e.g. the teenage children; the parents, grandmother and her favourite granddaughter; the boys; the girls – which have their own life within a wider system. Evan Imber-Black (1991) presents the family itself as a small system within a larger ecology, about which all the laws described above would apply. Person-centred counsellor Bob Lee, asked about family counselling, said he extends the concept of family '. . . way further. We are part of the human family all living together on "spaceship earth".' In conversation he discussed one effect of relational counselling as extending the parameters of how people think about the family they are in. Systems thinking allows ways of meeting individuals in context. It is a *gestalt* that sees the person as an organism which is always part of a larger organism.

It is important to note that practitioners of family therapy are by no means uniform in their application of the above principles. Further, a wooden, unimaginative version of systems thinking can be misleading and even dangerous. For example, a feminist critique of circular causality in contemporary western culture would reject the notion of equal responsibility in the case of physical abuse of a woman by a man. While authors such as Carter (1989, 1992) acknowledge that a shared system may certainly put pressures on both individuals that bring out their worst characteristics, they argue that the individual who physically abuses must be held accountable for his actions independent of their context. As an example of the potential for systems misunderstanding, early family therapists rigidly maintained that an individual's schizophrenic behaviour served the purpose of expressing family-wide dysfunction and would subside as the family became more congruent (Bateson et al., 1956). In light of biological discoveries of the last three decades (Efran et al., 1998), this thinking now seems one-sided. A family perspective would see all individuals within the family as mutually influencing and jointly struggling with common burdens. A person with schizophrenic symptoms (neither the person-centred approach nor most family approaches like to identify an individual with his symptoms!) is part of a family group, all of whom suffer and all of whom contribute to one another's suffering.

It may be said that family therapy and the person-centred approach both offer paradigms that are hopeful for persons in distress, but they derive these paradigms differently. The person-centred approach is deeply hopeful, based on reliance on the natural tendency of living organisms to move in a constructive and life-enhancing direction. The family therapy approach is hopeful, based on the enormous creative possibilities engendered by systems thinking.

Carl Rogers and systems thinking

Many of Carl Rogers' essays – 'Dealing with breakdowns in communication' (1961b) and 'A tentative formulation of a general law of interpersonal relationships' in *On Becoming a Person* (1961a) and his paper 'Person to Person: Parent and Adolescent' (1972b) – show his interest in the same dilemmas faced by relational counsellors. His essay, 'The implications of client-centered therapy for family life' (1961c), contains the following themes about persons living in relational systems:

- the importance of emotional expressiveness;
- the conviction that 'life can be lived on a real basis';
- the possibility of improvement in two-way communication;
- willingness for the other to be separate.

Rogers gave examples of clients who learned to tell their individual counsellor their most important thoughts and feelings, while assuming that they could never talk in such a way to those with whom they live. He believed that one outcome of good counselling was that clients, having less reason to be defensive, would be able to listen without judgement and distortion to those with whom they live. For example, he reports of a client, that '. . . as she had experienced in therapy the satisfaction of being herself, of voicing her deepest feelings, it became impossible for her to behave differently with her husband' (1961c: 317).

He felt that much trouble in family life is the result of unexpressed feelings which, when they sweep over a person, are 'inappropriate to the specific situation and hence seem to be unreasonable' (1961c: 318). He asserted that expression of all important feelings, positive as well as negative, would allow people not only to be closer, but to be more free from the overload of unexpressed feelings pouring out in time of crisis. His implied theory of family work was that it would begin with any one individual who changed her part in relationships in the direction of honesty, openness and directness. His writings exactly parallel Bowen's consistent assertions that profound family change begins when one individual takes 'the I position' (Anonymous, 1972: 118). Box 3.1 contains one example of the similarity between Rogers' work and a systems approach. Rogers' client realizes that her own actions contribute to the problem with which she is distressed. She is also aware of how her actions and demeanor (which she thought were caused by her mother's behaviour) were in turn affecting her own daughter's behaviour. Further, she realizes that if she makes a change in her own behaviour it will affect the whole system. Rogers details how his client's change in attitude opens the door to new experiences for her mother.

Box 3.1   Individual counselling begins a change in a whole system

In *On Becoming a Person* (1961d), Rogers shares a client's account of how she changed in relation to her elderly and seemingly helpless mother, towards whom she had great resentment – which to her horror she found reflected in the way her own daughter would refer to her grandmother (p. 324). His client tells of her own transformation, first of attitude and then of behaviour: 'Well I've made a stupendous discovery, that perhaps it's been my fault entirely in overcompensating to mother . . . in other words spoiling her.' So his client decides to not respond to her mother's emotional 'spells' in the way that she usually does. 'I didn't rush in and say, oh, I'm sorry and beg her to come back and I simply just ignored it. So in a few minutes, why she came back and sat down and was a little sulky but she was over it.'

His client starts doing more things from which she had previously refrained for fear her mother could not be left alone. She found a reasonable and safe time for her mother to be alone. 'She has a telephone by her bed . . .'

Her mother in turn reacts to positive news from a doctor in a way different from her usual withdrawal and depression: 'when she was faced with the fact that . . . her heart's as strong as a bull's, why she thought she may as well use it to have some fun with it. So that's fine.'

Rogers goes on to comment that the relationship was not only improved for his client but also for her mother, as his client found herself more and more able to experience positive feelings for her mother and to enjoy her: 'So that I noticed that yesterday when I was helping her get ready and so forth; I fixed her hair and there was the longest time I couldn't stand to touch her; and I was doing her hair in pin curls and so forth and I . . . it suddenly came to me, well now this doesn't bother me a bit; in fact it's kind of fun.'

Key concepts in relational counselling

In general, relational counsellors believe that we can better know how people feel if we also are able to *see* the objective situation in which they live. The following are ways of looking at couples and family experience that are frequently described in family therapy literature (see Minuchin, 1974, for the perspective of Structural Family Therapy, or more comprehensively, Gurman and Kniskern, 1991, *Handbook of Family Therapy*, volume 2). The reader may test how lively and informative these concepts are by applying them to any important period of her own development in her family of origin. They raise important questions about the objective external dimension of subjective experience.

Family rules

These are the unconscious habits of social living: repetitive patterns of communication and implicit norms about what is attended to and what is ignored – what is spoken and what must not be spoken. For example, the husband in a couple may be the only one who talks with his mother about important matters even though he is notoriously avoidant of negotiating complicated issues. It is more accepted that his wife and his mother both sit at home depressed over misunderstanding each other rather than talk directly to each other.

Developmental tasks

This concept refers to the way the life cycle can change the entire relational world of a family. For example, in a family, the physical and cognitive growth of teenagers or physical changes of mid-life can extensively change everyone's subjective world. In a couple, one partner's growing interest and success in a job outside the home can threaten family members' comfort and security even while it enhances his self-esteem and sense of purpose.

Environmental pressures

The counsellor may seek to understand the way cultural norms, the wider economic climate, or events at work or school can affect a couple or family. In the early days of family therapy, one of its founding fathers Nathan Ackerman was influenced by the correlation of children's school problems and their father's unemployment (Broderick and Schrader, 1991). As another example, Brown and Zimmer (1986) have written about the way that homophobia, external and internalized, may colour every aspect of the way a man may relate to his male partner and a female to her female partner.

Intergenerational patterns

The counsellor stays aware of how ways of acting and thinking reflect learning or attempts to unlearn the ways of one's family of origin. Person-centred family therapist Ned Gaylin has written a moving description of how, as a father in the present with his own son, he discovered himself living out a family scene that he vividly remembered experiencing as a child (1993: 196–7).

Boundary issues

The counsellor is encouraged to notice the way individual family members instinctively or habitually act around closeness and distance, openness and privacy. For example, a discussion about two brothers fighting may reveal that they *never* fight in the house without one of their parents becoming involved. In relation to boundaries, Minuchin (1974) coined the word *enmeshed* to describe a way of relating in which two or more people are so highly involved that there is little physical separation, permission for intellectual difference or tolerance for emotional distinctness. He developed the word *disengaged* to describe two or more people who appear emotionally cut off with little sharing, mutual empathy or concern. These concepts are useful for understanding ways in which couples formed from differing family cultures frustrate one another in expectations about the intensity of their involvement.

Alliances

This term refers to how included and supported people feel with other family members or how excluded and disconnected they feel in relation to others' perceived closeness. Alliances exist both in reality and in perception. In one family, a person may suffer greatly from the inability to share in an apparent natural compatibility that exists between two of her sisters. She may carry the self-concept 'outsider' into all her interactions. On the other hand, another person may inaccurately perceive closeness and alliances between family members who in fact are as alone and misunderstood as he is.

Hierarchy

It is important who is in charge of whom and for what reason or under what conditions; and how or if change is permitted. Therapists from a structural point of view are also very interested in incongruence between expected hierarchy and actual hierarchy. This is often particularly important in blended families: in one family a newcomer might assume that, since he is adult, he is in charge; in another family, he might assume that, since he is not father, he has no authority at all; and a third person, fearing conflict with all concerned, might give each family member different messages (Visher and Visher, 1987).

Cross-cultural impasses

The counsellor may listen to the way the meanings of words and events is shaped by each adult family member's historical experience. For example, some couples may live with the shadow of never feeling 'permission to marry' (Falicov, 1986) – that is, an undeclared half-heartedness in a relationship based on unspoken feelings of illegitimacy about choosing a partner outside their race, class or religion.

Unacknowledged loss

The counsellor may be aware of the impact of illness, traumatic events, death, failures or disappointment on seemingly unrelated communications and underlying family morale. For example, a woman's decision against a particular career because of the birth of a child may, if unspoken, haunt her and affect many seemingly unrelated transactions with partner and children.

It is not the counsellor's job to force the family into intellectual chatter about these issues, and even less to impose interpretations that reduce complex feelings to simple explanations. It may be the counsellor's job to carry awareness of internal and external influences that those caught inside a family whirlwind may not be able to access without her describing it. The work of Salvador Minuchin (1974; Minuchin and Nichols, 1993) and Jay Haley (1976) can give the reader a lively picture of ways in which these concepts are used in a very active therapy. Structural and strategic family therapists challenge family members, reframe the family definition of a problem, direct experiments in the session, assign homework (which often requires change in roles that affect hierarchy and boundaries), and take responsibility for instigating change in a system which has become incongruent. Says Minuchin, not without a sense of humour, 'People come to us and say: "We are in trouble." The therapist says, "I am an expert in meddling in people's lives." And they say, "Okay will you help us out?"' (Minuchin and Nichols, 1993).

Relational counsellors are active

Family and couples counsellors usually do more, say more, ask more questions, initiate more interactions, and offer more suggestions than

individual therapists – and certainly more than person-centred individual therapists. They also may ask clients to postpone some
behaviours, for example: not beginning a counselling session with a
long recitation of a teenager's faults by the parents. They sometimes
change the direction of other interactions, for example: asking for
comments on an argument, rather than sitting patiently through its
course. They open sessions, close sessions, and in general are heard
from more than most individual counsellors. In individual counselling, counsellor activity may distract from a client's freedom to focus
on feelings and meanings at the edge of her awareness. In relational
counselling, the activity of the counsellor *may free* clients from the
restrictions of rule-governed, repetitive sequences.

Couples and family counsellor activity may be seen in the following ways.

The counsellor structures the sessions, especially at the beginning. Because
more than one person is sharing the business of the counselling hour,
the counsellor invites them to make sense of what their common
purpose might be. He deals with when they will leave and when or if
they will come back; he addresses why he meets with whole families
or couples and what they might expect of him. This can be all quite
simple – it can be covered by an introduction, the answering of
questions, the asking of questions, the setting of limits. Paradoxically,
by defining the meeting in terms that can be easily understood, the
counsellor avoids making her unspoken expectations more central to
the meeting than the family's needs, dilemmas and hopes. If the
counsellor fails to clarify her purpose and role, the sessions could be
dominated by clients' expression of confusion and insecurity.
Similarly, the counsellor encourages room for people to finish what
they are saying or invites commentary from silent members.
Ironically, a relational counsellor may be active for the very same
reason that an individual counsellor may be inactive: for the sake of
each person's freedom to find her own truest voice and intention.

*The counsellor, in practising multi-directional partiality (see Chapter 1),
solicits and facilitates the stories of all the family members.* He has a
relationship with every family member and he must not take for
granted that his presence will be felt except by lively exchanges (or
respectful acknowledgment of unreadiness for exchange). Answering
the question of how she was different in couples than in individual
work, Joyce Marx, a therapist with 40 years' experience said '[in
couples work] I engage. There is lots more life in me.' In describing
her first session behaviour, she had emphasized: '. . . respect for the
major decision a couple has made to come and be so exposed. I work
to make a connection with each – to make clear that I'm not going to

take sides, that I'll be non-judgemental, that I'll try to see both points of view, that I'll give both a chance to talk.' For her the core conditions of effective therapy need to be actively communicated in this medium.

The counsellor meets the family in a way that comes naturally to her. She reacts to the family drama with personal involvement. She is interested, can be moved, is amused, is sad, joins in the family conversation when asked or when a feeling or perception becomes urgent, and retains her ability to be observer. The counsellor is a witness who cares but does not attempt to control. Veteran family therapist Breffni Barrett told me: 'A good family therapist is a strong character – very involved, but doesn't take charge. You are a good grandparent.'

The counsellor reflects on the interactions of the family. He reacts as someone who is 'in' the family enough to have something of the family's experience but out of it enough to offer perspective. The counsellor models reflection and curiosity rather than single-mindedness and certainty. In the medium of family therapy, like the medium of group therapy, the counsellor invites reflection on dimensions other than one's subjective experience. If 'felt meanings' (Gendlin, 1970) are central to individual counselling, meanings that are *seen* and *heard* are the focus of couples and family work. As in group, couples and family members surrender their unspoken interpretations in favour of more clarity and objectivity. Family members' awareness of any of these dimensions can give more richness and complexity (to use a phrase of Jay Haley, 1973) to their understanding of self and others.

Relational counsellors *reframe*

This practice, which may be defined as *offering a different perspective which changes the meaning of an event or process* (usually but not always in more positive terms), is frequently used in family and couples therapy. Family therapist James Framo has written:

> Probably the most valuable technique used by family therapists has been the *reframe*. Although it was not a new concept (an analytic interpretation is a reframe) nonetheless the reframe has been most usefully employed by family therapists and has, when used skillfully, been most effective in bringing about change. By relabeling noxious or even destructive

behaviors as benign in intent, by offering a way of seeing events in a different light and by recasting motives, fixed beliefs about one's self or others can undergo enduring transformations. (Framo, 1996)

'Reframing' covers a range of behaviours, from highlighting an over-looked aspect of a situation – 'in any event, Joe's suspension has done away with the notion that he is an entirely predictable little brother' – to a planned paradoxical intervention – 'I think you may need to fight more in order to revive your more youthful expressiveness.'

The use of reframing derives from the assumption that *the meaning a social group gives to an event or way of being helps create that event.* Further, any change in the perceived meaning of an event or way of being can, for a family or individual in distress, offer liberation and a strong source of motivation for cooperation and change. Salvador Minuchin has said: 'We are paid to expand the reality of people who are stuck' (Minuchin and Nichols, 1993). For example, in a fierce argument about honesty in a business plan between a couple who are about to be married, the counsellor might say: 'I hear a strong attempt by both of you to make sure your real voices get heard in this marriage.'

This example, from my own practice, offered the couple in question a perspective which allowed both to have strong feelings without the burden of having to be right and having to view the other as wrong. The comment arose naturally in my tracking the course of the conversation in its meaning for each of the speakers, rather than judging who might be right regarding the content of the discussion. That is: *I did hear it.* I didn't just think it was a good idea to have heard it. It is not a standard response I give to couples to put a good light on their arguments. It is a *genuine* response even while it is a suggestion about another level of understanding the conversation. In the spirit of a person-centred approach, it is not a correction. Indeed, if one or both members of the couple felt misunderstood or that their conversation was being watered down or sweetened up, the response would fall flat or be dropped in the face of their contradiction. There is no evidence that in any of his therapeutic work Carl Rogers ever intentionally reframed anything. In fact he has said:

At any rate it's been very much my experience in therapy that one does not need to supply motivation toward the positive or toward the constructive. That exists in the individual. In other words, if we can release what is most basic in the individual, then it will be constructive. (Kirschenbaum and Henderson, 1990: 58)

Rogers felt that, trusted and well accompanied by a counsellor, people would naturally move toward a more complex, process-oriented, acceptant way of looking at things (Rogers, 1959). *That reframing is a natural human function was central to his system; the counsellor as reframer was not.* (Remember 'Do We Need a Reality?' in *A Way of Being*, Rogers, 1980?)

In the way reframing takes place lies the whole possibility of a dialogue between the person-centred approach and schools of thought such as *Strategic Family Therapy*. Is the therapist a self-proclaimed wizard who, knowing what is best, gets people out of their distress using means outside their awareness? Or is the therapist a fully engaged partner who, with a wink or other signal indicating the spirit of play, invites absurd solutions to absurd problems?

Rogers' long-time associate John K. Wood told me a story about his brother complaining to him of a lifelong fear of heights that was severely restricting his business because he was unable to fly on airplanes. John said that he told him, 'You mean to say that you can't do two things at once: be afraid and fly on an airplane.' His brother listened and the next time he saw John reported that he had taken himself to the tallest hotel in San Diego and ridden up the elevator on the outside of the building again and again. He repeated to himself: 'I can do two things at once: be afraid and ride on this elevator.' From then on, he flew on airplanes without excessive anxiety. John offered the story after reading some articles on strategic therapy and a draft of this chapter. He had not been pursuing any strategy or implanting any paradox. He told his brother what he thought and his brother, in a state of receptivity, did something different. John's intention was to speak helpfully to his brother's dilemma and in so doing he added a different possibility. Jay Haley once said when asked about anorexia that he 'wouldn't let that be the problem. A family can't cure anorexia [an alienating disease concept]. They can solve the problem of a child's refusing to eat [a practical matter of family life].' Strategic therapy emphasizes empowerment by searching for a problem definition that allows one to take action on one's problems. As long as John's brother was trying to overcome the fear of heights he would not succeed; once he heard his dilemma as a difficult but endurable task he was empowered.

Why do many relational counsellors actively reframe? Perhaps it is because people often come in pairs or whole families for one purpose: *to get a conversation started which they want but feel they cannot have without losing their integrity.* The counsellor's presence in itself represents the notion that a conversation is possible. Even the minimal counsellor activity of saying, 'I wonder what you, Bob, might have to say about what Marilyn just shared,' assumes that there is more than one opinion that may be listened to and that there is at least a part of Marilyn that wants to hear it. In meeting two or more people who have temporarily divided reality into right and wrong, good and bad, hopeful and hopeless, the therapist may share a different perspective, which if perceived as authentic, can allow for a different kind of conversation. In individual counselling the counsellor's empathy and lack of judgement may facilitate a client's natural reframing process. In relational counselling, the counsellor's reframing may be an additional step toward *disarming judgement so that empathy may be possible*. Box 3.2 presents reflection on the way reframing can allow clients to release rigid assumptions that block their understanding.

Box 3.2   Reframing as a bridge

On the day he loses his job, a man may say to his wife who tries to comfort him, 'I just want to take a walk by myself', and thereby hurt her deeply. As she understands it, he must not love and value her very much to exclude her at such a vital moment in his life. He, on the other hand, may have one of many motivations for seeking aloneness – a sense of needing to repair himself alone so that he does not feel ashamed in her presence; the habit, long established, of reaching inside for steadying thoughts that another's comforting voice would block; a fear that he cannot be loved while feeling weak.

He may also be desperately afraid of being controlled by his most loved other and fear that her control would be strengthened by his allowing her to comfort him when his own sense of personal control is low. Even this fear is not in itself about her, but about his own habitual defensive structure. She, sensing this, may be angry with him even as she understands his fear, and may be angry with herself for letting her feelings of exclusion begin to become more important than his original distress. His desire to be by himself to heal may be accompanied by anger displaced from his predicament onto her. He may put more energy into insisting that he be left alone and then be ashamed that he is excluding her and knowingly hurting her feelings.

The counsellor may be aware of the impact of dozens of such incidents on the ease and closeness of a relationship. Without 'trying to supply motivation toward the positive', she may suggest that the couple suffer from a *common source of distress* that lives not in their characters but in the nature of their relationship independent of their intentions. She may ask if they were both suffering from the fact that one partner's first instinct in crisis was to reach out and that the other's was to push away; and that these instincts have a life of their own independent of the relationship. This is a reframe of her paradigm that 'he doesn't want me' and his that 'she won't let me be myself'.

Reframing may make sense in couples and family counselling in a way in which it would not make sense in individual counselling. *Relational counselling has a dependence on the cognitive, which may, at times, precede the emotional* (see Zimring, 1995 for a discussion of the presence of attention to client meanings as well as feelings in Rogers' work). If I am convinced that my partner's actions mean that she doesn't value me, my feelings of hurt, loss, fear or even anger will be stirred and directed in a way inevitably different than if I understand her actions in terms of her own distress independent of me.

The relational counsellor has two interests at once. He is forever reliant on clients' sharing of 'gut reactions' as the royal road to effective intimate communication. The person who shares his immediate feelings in a spirit of trust creates the softening which allows people to live compatibly in the face of even very complex differences. *Quite another matter, however, is the 'gut reaction' in which a much feared meaning is imposed upon another's behaviour and blocks out listening to alternative meanings independent of the hearer's mindset.* Hugh and Gayle Prather capture this well: 'Except for some serial killers, most people are too selfish to devote many of their waking thoughts to how to make someone else miserable, but some couples feel that this may be so for their partners' (Prather and Prather, 1988).

The reader may look at the following continuum and place herself close to the description that matches her usual practice. She may then reflect upon some of the interpersonal relationships with which she has been involved personally or professionally. What level of coun- sellor reframe may be necessary in order for conversation to take place?

- The counsellor is present and open, with a highly developed trust that as conversation develops people naturally reframe their predicaments.
- The counsellor actively facilitates dialogue, so that, in an atmos- phere where people have the safety to share what they think and feel, a situation is reframed through fuller disclosure.
- The counsellor is present, involved in the dialogue, open to his intuition. He may share metaphors, ideas that seem relevant to the relationship dilemma. He participates and reframes by trusting his own felt reactions.
- The counsellor reframes for the sake of interpreting one person's words to another in the most positive way that is compatible with congruence.
- The counsellor reframes by what she responds to and by what she ignores: highlighting 'softening' responses such as 'when you did that I felt hurt and like you weren't interested' and paying little attention to accusatory, interpretive language.

- The counsellor reframes actively, staying close to the meaning of the data but showing a perspective that allows all parties to stay on the same side against a common dilemma.
- The counsellor reframes actively, sometimes deliberately para-doxically, sometimes independent of what he actually believes to be true, strategically seeking a certain effect.

In my career, I have occupied all parts of the above continuum, including, I'm afraid, a brief unsuccessful visit to the extreme strategic side. Sometimes it is difficult for the counsellor to see how her way of being may be seen from outside – video review and supervision are needed to seek objectivity. *Couples and families influence how the counsellor may behave.* For example, a couple in the extreme of anxiety and anger may require active reframing to even keep the two people in the same room. Of course the counsellor may be able to invite the clients to be the prime movers in the reframe which, at its heart, is simply the movement from a rigid one-sided way of perceiving a situation to a more fluid way of engaging with it. A question such as the following may lead to a client's reframing her words so that her partner can hear them: 'If you Michael could sit back for a moment, could you, Celia, just engage with me and tell me what in all of this upsets you the most?'

In reference to reframing, person-centred counsellors may ask some of the following questions:

- If I were a client in couples or family therapy, what level of reframing would allow me to feel respected and trusted by the counsellor?
- Are there circumstances or meetings with significant others in which this might change?
- When is a reframe the forcing of a perception rather than the revelation of another possibility?
- Does a counsellor reframe because of an unconditional positive regard that instinctively sees the constructive in all client situations, or because of a lack of unconditional positive regard which leads to the assumption of responsibility for changing meanings for a client?
- How can reframing become a skill that is modelled, shared and otherwise learned by the client(s) as counselling progresses?

Box 3.3 Reframing out of control

Every counselling approach contains seeds of the ridiculous within. At his worst a person-centred counsellor's responses might become predictable – one too many 'mmm-hmm' or a muted 'you sound really angry' to someone who has just stood up and yelled that he was about to carve out the counsellor's entrails. Similarly, relational counsellors may become so good at reframing that people despair of ever getting a direct reaction from them. Thus:

- angry judgemental speech may automatically become an 'attempt to be heard at a deeper level than conventional attempts to please';
- carelessness could be translated to 'a loving attempt to model freedom from inessentials';
- longwindedness is, of course, 'a really thorough manner of speech';
- a couple locked in icy silence for two months may be described as 'taking a much needed moratorium from conversation'; and
- a person unemployed and inactive for over a year is 'in the cave of quiet creativity'.

Relational counsellors ask questions

The family or couples counsellor may ask many questions. In individual counselling, the earliest client-centred research favoured the giving up of questioning along with other indications of counsellor authority and control (Kirschenbaum and Henderson, 1990). In his analysis of successful individual interviewing, Rogers consistently pointed out the way counsellor questions or comments would interfere with the client's natural and effective process (Kirschenbaum and Henderson, 1990: 88–108). In relational counselling, facilitating rather than information seeking questions may give clients a way to bypass interference and feel safe enough to reflect freely rather than defend rigidly.

The following are common categories of relational counsellor questions.

Housekeeping questions

Questions for the beginning and end of sessions; questions that clarify goals, that invite participation, that take care of the aspect of relational counselling that is a meeting. 'What brings you, Philip, to this session besides your wife having asked you to come?' 'How are we doing so far? Are we talking about what you hoped we would talk about?'

Facilitating questions

Questions that organize discussion; that focus persons' attention on the same issue; that link what is currently being said to earlier interaction; that clarify or reframe so that an issue does not carry the burden of one person's frame of reference directed against another. 'What are you hearing when Marie speaks?' 'Is there any part of this that reflects your own experience?'

Mediating questions

Questions that invite accurate listening; that give order in chaotic argument; that focus attention on genuine feelings, opinions and wishes rather than accusations, projected fears and threats. The counsellor is not in charge of sanitizing exchanges so that one person's hard truth is taken out of focus. He is, however, often asked to provide a medium in which people can be heard and can hear without feeling they have to lose either their integrity or connection or both. Person-centred counsellor Arlene Wiltburger sometimes asks clients in conflict what the intention is behind their argument. A 17-year-old girl's intention may be 'to do something on her own in which she has to make her own decisions' – an intention with which her mother may well agree. Her mother's intention may be that the girl be safe – with which the girl may agree (Wiltburger, 1985).

Narrative therapy

While on the subject of asking *questions* of clients I need to give a brief introduction to *narrative therapy*, an imaginative approach which often uses questions for dialogue with frustrated, discouraged and blaming families and couples. David Epston, co-originator of narrative therapy, has reflected '. . . we must forever be realizing that people are multi-storied, just as our stories of culture and psychology are. For instance, what would have happened if Carl Rogers' work had become the privileged psychological text rather than Freud's? It would seem that we would have a totally different psychological world' (Madigan, 1994).

Narrative therapy, founded by David Epston and Michael White (White and Epston, 1990) offers a unique way of discovering grounds for unconditional positive regard in family and couples work. Narrative therapists frequently ask questions in order to expand the awareness of distressed families. '[We] ask questions to generate experience rather than to gather information' (Freedman and Combs, 1996: 113). Their questions challenge *problem saturated stories* which often offer individual members no alternative but to blame or lose hope in themselves or in one another. Two ways are described below in which narrative therapists collaborate with families to make possible a story that has fewer villains and less dead ends.

1. They externalize the problem: that is, they find a way to distinguish the persons in the family from the problem that baffles them. For example, a word like *delinquency* may be used to describe and personify a force against which the whole family struggles. '*Delinquency* thinks you should believe you can never have a job because you can never allow anyone to tell you what to do.' Or, '*Delinquency* tells you to never just enjoy your son because any sign of approval will encourage him to be in more trouble.'
2. They use questions to encourage reflection on unnoticed resources in the family. For example, they identify, call attention to and thoroughly investigate the meaning of 'unique outcomes' (White and Epston, 1990) or unexpected and unlooked-for moments in which an individual or family acted effectively, cooperatively, freely or otherwise as if the problem did not exist. In discussing unique outcome, the family organizes around a different story than the one that brought them to counselling. For example, 'On that occasion, what made it possible for you to not act like the "parent of a delinquent" but as someone who had a right to enjoy his son?' 'When you came home that night how did you know that you were going to be able to stand up to delinquency by talking to your sister rather than running away?'

The reader may see Freedman and Combs (1996) for a wide variety of questions used in order to facilitate dialogue. In Chapter 10 I give an example of my own use of David Epston's practice of writing letters to clients. Each person-centred counsellor will have to decide whether the concepts of externalized problems and unique outcome and the techniques of evocative questions and the naming of dilemmas will serve more to empower clients or will highlight the counsellor's role at the expense of trust in the client's own process. In my relational work, I have sometimes found the narrrative style to be the only way that I could communicate with clients and be both congruent and acceptant. Sometimes I have needed a way to talk about parents' behaviours without getting caught up in scolding them, however covertly! At other times, a narrative approach has kept me from joining parents in their anger and frustration with their children. The use of story in the narrative mode can offer a means of telling a truth without targeting an individual or family for blame. Narrative therapists in family work may draw on the same resources of intuition and imagery described by Rogers (1980) and Mearns (1997).

Person-centred counsellors and activity, reframing and asking questions

How can the person-centred approach allow us to reflect on these descriptions of approaches to relational therapy? A client in couples and family counselling has at least four concerns that must be addressed whether or not they are articulated:

1. How can I *get in* the conversation, or how can my more withdrawn or reluctant partner or children get in?
2. How can I talk about our *deepest conflicts* and keep my self-respect and not diminish the self-respect of my significant others?
3. How can we have this conversation so that it is *fair* and feels fair?
4. How can we have this conversation *safely* so that our relationship grows rather than deteriorates?

Whether or not a counsellor is active, reframes or asks questions is less important than what his doing so says about his belief in the clients. Facilitator activity can implicitly carry the assumption that the clients would not take responsibility for that activity or a more useful one themselves. Facilitator inactivity can sometimes convey non-caring, lack of awareness of the unique dilemma of a relationship, or rigidity of approach. The effective counsellor in relational counselling is less central to the clients, for whom relationship with spouse, child, mother or brother is very much foreground, even while paradoxically she is more active and takes more initiatives.

Carl Rogers was always aware of how easy it is for a counsellor, for the most benevolent of reasons, to substitute her own need to be useful, significant or intelligent for an attitude which allows the client to unfold at his own pace. The heart of Rogers' work was that: 'He tried to listen and understand *every single thing* the client was telling him . . . the client felt understood by an honest person' (Wood, 1995). He rarely asked clients questions. He tended instead to ask *himself* questions like: 'Can I be in some way which will be perceived by the other person as trustworthy . . . ?' 'Can I let myself experience positive attitudes toward this person . . . ?' (Rogers, 1980). His reflection: '. . . unless I had a need to demonstrate my own cleverness and learning, I would do better to rely on the client for the direction of movement in the process' (Rogers, 1967) is a challenge to be echoed in all meaning-ful supervision (see Shein, 1987, for a similar statement in the world of business consultation). The counsellor who indiscriminately takes action, reframes or asks questions can be as constricted as the coun-sellor who feels she will not act in almost any circumstances. Chapter 4 will discuss the core conditions as they may be seen in relational counselling. The reader may reflect on the richness which these con-ditions have to offer the activity, reframing and questions of the person-centred relational counsellor.

Relational Counselling and the Six Core Conditions of the Person-Centred Approach

In his 1957 article, Carl Rogers set an agenda for all therapists by asserting that the presence of six core conditions was the necessary and sufficient means to creating a therapeutic outcome, independent of method utilized by the therapist. Person-centred counsellors are familiar with the ways that these core conditions may come alive in individual counselling, in group counselling, in training and in education. Ned Gaylin (1989) has written eloquently about their application to family therapy. Similarly, many non-person-centred couples and family therapists attribute significant influences to these concepts. Johnson and Greenberg (1994a) credit Rogers' (1951) influence on their *emotionally focused couples therapy*. Duncan, Hubble and Miller (1997b) sum up dozens of studies on efficacy in therapy by asserting that client factors and the relationship with a therapist with perceived qualities of acceptance, realness and empathy were significantly more influential on outcome than was technique. What follows are reflections on the way in which these core conditions may be understood in the context of family and couples counselling.

The counsellor is in psychological contact with the client

'All that is intended by this first condition is to specify that the two people are to some degree in contact, that each makes some perceived difference in the experiential field of the other' (Rogers, 1957).

In relational counselling, psychological contact must be made between the counsellor and all of the persons who attend a session. The counsellor should presume unevenness of contact, in that no two people will have the same openness to meet her and she will not be able to show exactly the same degree of openness to each. Nevertheless, she must, especially in the beginning of the relationship, make contact with clients, attending in such a way that *they all feel received by someone who is potentially their own counsellor rather than someone belonging to significant others*. There is also a need for the counsellor to be perceived as in contact with a family or a couple as a whole, in addition to his connection with each individual.

The spirit of person-centred individual counselling allows the client unlimited permission to engage the counsellor at his own pace. Silence, hesitation, even small talk, soliloquies or lengthy reports of the blameworthiness of others are received without judgement. In fact, the client-centred counsellor in individual counselling is presenting the client with what is ultimately the biggest challenge: another person who takes him seriously, who reflects back whatever he expresses and who ultimately lets him meet himself.

Frequently in relational counselling one of the clients will be seemingly more motivated, more at home with counselling and more verbal and forthcoming. The counsellor has the task of not only listening to that person, but also of connecting with the more silent members of a family or couple. Similarly, the counsellor must not only listen to those persons who initially seem more congruent, more able to speak for themselves, more responsible, but also to the person who at first shows few or none of these qualities. For example:

> *Counsellor*: What brings you here Michael?
> *Michael*: Well, just look at her and you can see. She is flirting, rude, shows no respect for me; does little around the house. She just wants me to support her and to give nothing in return. (The counsellor may feel momentarily like trying another profession! How can he meet Michael in any congruent way that does not drive either him or the wife he is describing out of the room?)
> *Counsellor*: Michael, it won't be my job to try to judge Jackie or you. I want to work with both of you on what you each would like to talk about. It looks like you are starting off with some things that are making you angry.

The counsellor has more than one task: he is meeting Michael and finding out what he wants. He is also, in whatever he says to Michael, making his first contact with Michael's wife, Jackie. In this example, the counsellor both acknowledges Michael's feelings and also frames his job as counsellor – to hear and try to understand feelings, but not to join any judgement on another client. In individual counselling he might have simply responded by something like: 'You are really angry. You feel your wife really mistreats you . . .'

Later, after Michael has described his frustration with the ways that Jackie has changed, his feeling of being taken for granted and his desire that she return to the way she was when they first married, the counsellor turns to Jackie.

Counsellor: And why did you come today, Jackie?

Jackie: Well he's right. If he's saying I've changed, he's right. I'm not the same little mouse he married five years ago. I've got a life and I'm a person.

(Michael interrupts): See what I mean? That's all I get from her.

Counsellor: Let me keep staying with what Jackie has to say, Michael. Then I'll get back to hearing what you want me to know.

The counsellor is doing a number of things at once. He is reassuring Michael that his concerns are important. He is also looking for a way of proceeding that acknowledges Michael without joining him against Jackie. He will also need to meet Jackie without joining her in a quickly formed alliance against Michael. He is simply taking a stand in favour of Jackie being allowed to get into the conversation (while hoping that Michael can tolerate this). He is active as a counsellor may need to be while clients are learning how to express themselves without driving away their significant others.

The relational counsellor is sometimes like the facilitator in a training programme. She accepts individuals as they are, but may make explicit certain structural expectations that go with the *medium* they enter. Michael is welcome in counselling just as he is, but the counselling itself demands a minimal ability to engage in give-and-take with another. It may sometimes be helpful for the counsellor to describe the process, as much in terms of her own behaviour as of what clients are allowed or not allowed to do.

Counsellor: I'm going to be finding out from each of you what brings you to counselling and what you hope to gain from being here. I will probably be going back and forth between you for a while, with nobody finishing everything they want to say completely, so that everybody gets a chance to get involved in the session. I may interrupt from time to time so that we are all in on getting this picture of what you want.

This kind of explicit process description is usually not required in individual counselling, in which most individuals quickly adapt to the counsellor's openness to listen. In relational counselling this minimal courtesy may be the only way to make psychological contact with a family member brought to counselling who has no idea what to expect.

In the spirit of the person-centred approach, there is another dimension to psychological contact. Prior to his demonstration interviews, Carl Rogers used to take a moment to concentrate before turning his attention toward a client in a demonstration. He maintained that he entered another state of consciousness in which everything else faded into the background except for the client (Rogers, 1979). His clients reported that his concentrated attention felt extraordinary (writer's observation). Box 4.1 describes some of the questions and assumptions that shape my way of giving psychological attention to each individual in relational counselling.

Box 4.1 Individualized personal contact

In a family or couples context the counsellor's interest and personal attention would be shown in noticing each person in a family and attending not just to what they say, but to nonverbal cues they may be giving her. The counsellor may ask herself the following types of questions:

- What will this young client think of being in the spotlight? How much will he tolerate others talking about him and asking him questions?
- Is this young child able to participate in the discussion? Should I offer her something to draw or play with or see what her parents do?
- How much can this wife tolerate my listening to her husband's lengthy talking before she thinks I am joining him, man to man, in a project to improve her?
- Should I let this angry argument run its course or should I interrupt by active listening or other structuring or anxiety-reducing activity?
- Is this couple more likely to feel stifled by my intervention or abandoned by my silence? (This is a major question requiring the counsellor's attention to multiple cues in the early stages of counselling. As counselling progresses, the clients may be able to inform the counsellor more explicitly and may be less interested in the counsellor's expectations.)

Over time I have found myself making the following assumptions:

- Teenagers may perceive silence and lack of direction as threatening and judging of them (until they know and trust the counsellor).
- Not enough interaction on the therapist's part can also enable parents already trapped in their dominance to fill the silence with the same blaming monologues they know have never helped.
- An angry client, who initiated the counselling, may get a chance to speak his or her mind in such a way that a reluctant partner has doubts about counselling confirmed.

- An angry couple may fill the session with a fight that leaves each feeling more discouraged and unheard.
- Unclarified accusations may remain in clients minds and decrease their trust of one another.

The clients are in a state of incongruence

'The first person whom we shall term the client, is in a state of incongruence, being vulnerable or anxious . . .'. (Rogers, 1957)

Incongruence refers to a person's inability to acknowledge part of reality because it would contradict her self-concept. Rogers (1957) gives an example, relevant to family therapy, of a mother who cannot become aware that she is reluctant to let her grown son leave home. Instead she develops vague physical symptoms. In family counselling, the presenting problem is frequently reflective of a split between family members' actual experience and the concept of the experience, which they maintain to themselves as well as to one another. A classic example of such incongruence is a parent or spouse maintaining that he loves a family member while showing physical and behavioural signs of dislike and disgust. (This has been analysed in the description of the famous double bind theory in Bateson et al., 1956.)

The examples above describe the incongruence of individual family members, but sometimes incongruence extends to the entire family or system. Many families live with the illusion that their lives are going on as usual when there has been an event that has fundamentally changed the nature of their connection. The most common example is the effect of the birth of a first child on the relationship of a couple. The child's presence, beginning in pregnancy, changes the amount of time, attention, money, privacy, rest, peace and quiet, freedom and sexual spontaneity which characterize the relationship. The child does this for a significant amount of time (usually 18 years or more)! Even if the child does not have a particularly demanding or intrusive nature or difficulties requiring special attention, her presence alone may stir up unexpected emotions in the parents or their extended family. New parents can change and see one another change, but not acknowledge the effects of those differences on their relationship. This incongruence later manifests itself in a vague sense of frustration or a not-so-vague sense of blame. Box 4.2 contains examples of unspoken change. It is quite common to see a couple in which each member is withholding of affection or attention from the other while demanding that the other give more love and attention. Incongruence in this sense means, at best, a lack of a sense of perspective (to say nothing of humour) and at worst a loss of a sense of responsibility for one's own part in a deteriorating relationship.

Box 4.2   Incongruence and life change

The following are examples of unacknowledged changes that result in incongruence in a couple's implicit contract with one another:

- At the beginning of the relationship it was understood that the couple would talk and listen equally to each other's troubles every day. At the time of counselling only one has the habit of talking to a resentfully listening other; equality of airtime was suspended without discussion.
- At the beginning of the relationship it was understood that each would be an equal partner in decisions about use of money or child raising. As one member of a couple became more the breadwinner and received much confirming attention outside the home, the other became more and more hesitant to assert a role in money management or sense of ownership of the common household.
- At the beginning of the relationship it was assumed that one member of a couple was the leader and teacher and the other the willing follower and learner. At the time of counselling one member feels overburdened and taken for granted while the other feels patronized and kept in a box.
- At the beginning of the relationship it was assumed that one member's family would be the closest and would be a welcome community in which the couple would find their place. At the time of counselling, one member of the couple feels stifled, trapped and controlled by the other's family of origin.
- At the time of the coming of a child it was understood that unconditional love of that person would always be a constant and would have precedence over any parental guidance or correction. At the time of counselling, personalized criticism, argument or frosty silence has become the dominant way of relating between parent and child.

Incongruence is not caused directly by change in a family's structure, dynamics or developmental stage. *Changes are inevitable and the adjustment to life events is a sign of family health and strength.* Incongruence, rather, has to do with the inability of family members to talk about change and become aware of their reaction to it. *It is also, I believe, common even for loving and intelligent families to drift away from open and continuous acknowledgement of change.* Some fortunate families have or create opportunities for non-defensive conversations that correct what seems a natural trend. For other couples and families, the presence of a counsellor provides the safety and confidence to step back from an incongruence that frustrates, confuses and ultimately divides a relationship.

Some couples are incongruent by being unaware that their own way of talking and acting co-creates the negative words and treatment they receive from their partner. For example, a man may say: 'All she does is criticize me. When I married her she was sweet and positive. Now she's turned into her mother – worse than her mother – and now she only cares about putting me down.' The speaker, seemingly wishing for kinder words, is behaviourally 'pulling for' or evoking more angry critical defensive words from his partner (see Johnson and Greenberg, 1994a, for an excellent discussion of this).

Incongruent in a similar way, a woman may say, 'I know for a *fact* that he has stopped loving me. Just admit it, will you? All I want is for you to admit that you don't find me attractive anymore.' Under some conditions, this statement may be seen as congruent and an attempt to genuinely clear the air. Frequently, however, such statements are made in hopes of forcing a denial and are an attempt to gain reassurance.

The counsellor knows that incongruence is a natural event that has many causes and is a burden shared by all members of a family or couple. Understanding that incongruence is a predicament rather than a choice based on incompetence or ill will, sets the stage for the acceptant atmosphere that allows clients to become more congruent.

The counsellor is congruent

The second person whom we shall term the therapist, is congruent or integrated in the relationship. . . . [The therapist] should be, within the confines of this relationship, a congruent genuine, integrated person. It means that within the relationships he is freely and deeply himself, with his actual experience accurately represented by his awareness of himself. It is the opposite of presenting a facade, either knowingly or unknowingly.' (Rogers, 1957)

Congruence as not being up to something

Family therapist Carl Whitaker, whom Rogers credited as influencing his own use of the word congruence to describe this condition (Kirschenbaum, 1979: 196), once asked a severely disturbed client who had improved dramatically what it was that made the difference. The young man responded that it was an afternoon when 'nobody was up to anything' (Framo, 1981: 152).

Let us not pretend that there is no paradox here. On one level, of course a counsellor *is* up to something. Why else would someone go to a designated certified person, often pay money and have hope that a disturbing family condition will be relieved? The counsellor is certainly up to being helpful, being available and offering a way of doing things that has been helpful for others. However, the counsellor is *not* up to being secretive, mystifying, having an agenda that is kept from the clients. The counsellor does not 'attempt to portray' (Mearns, 1994a) a role of benevolence, confidence, sublime indifference or even of realness. He is transparent as much as possible, allowing the clients to feel safe and not having to defend themselves against manipulation.

The teenagers I see may know I want them to go to school, be generous and not just seek immediate gratification. The couples I counsel may know I generally wish that they would pay attention to each other and treat each other with respect. The parents I meet may know that I wish they would listen more and lecture less. The families who are my clients may know I wish they would develop a spirit of imagination and experimentation rather than one of rigidity and sameness. I do not have to conceal my own nature, including my values, as long as my primary intention is to fully understand the clients' nature and values. As a counsellor I can take what family therapist Murray Bowen calls an '"I" stand' (Bowen, 1978) based on my perspective, not on a claim to know what is best. Because the clients know I have opinions, they can meet me in dialogue; disagree with me; define their own values in contrast with mine; and learn comfort with their own ability to set their own course.

Congruence as awareness and openness

To Rogers, the term congruence referred to three levels: being aware of what he was experiencing; having his outer physical presence express what he was aware of; and finally being willing to disclose to the client any repeating significant experience (Rogers, 1980). In another place he describes congruence as being acceptant of himself and trusting that what 'rises up in me' will be relevant to the therapy enterprise:

> Now, acceptantly to be what I am, in this sense and to permit this to show through to the other person is the most difficult task I know . . . But to

realize that this is my task has been most rewarding because it has helped me to find what has gone wrong with interpersonal relationships which have become snarled and to put them on a constructive track again. (quoted in Kirschenbaum and Henderson, 1990: 120)

In family counselling, the counsellor may get pulled into strong opinions about right and wrong that only his awareness and non-defensiveness will keep from becoming a presumptuous interference. I might say to a client: 'I suddenly started to feel like a salesman with you. I think I'm trying to talk you into not moving out. What does it sound like to you when I say this?'

An admission of bias conveys respect for the client, while confirming the counselling itself as a meeting between complex human beings. The counsellor has the position: 'I am here to do my best, not to come up with a perfect solution to this family's problems.' The counsellor joins in with the family conversation and begins to have feelings related to the family. His interest and agreement with family members will never be uniform. What he offers the meeting is his humanity, along with his awareness of his humanity. His feelings are for him a trustworthy indicator of what is happening with the family. He may feel fear; he may feel worry. He may, in the midst of what seems to be a disastrous situation, feel confidence and even appreciation. Aware of the possibilities of the therapeutic meeting, he may be freer than the family members to not react in a stereotyped way. The reactions of a congruent outsider who is experiencing the couple or family freshly can increase the security and self-respect of all present. For example, to a couple in the middle of a repetitive quarrel a counsellor once said: 'Let me give you what keeps staying with me from what you said ten minutes ago. Beverly, you just said: "I've been depressed all my adult life." Did I hear that right?' In response, Beverly became thoughtful and spoke of something different than her accusations. Her partner's eyes filled with tears and he said: 'I know how hard this has been for her,' instead of continuing with his more usual defensive speech.

The counsellor experiences unconditional positive regard for the clients

To the extent that the therapist finds himself experiencing a warm acceptance of each aspect of the client's experience as being a part of that client, he is experiencing unconditional positive regard . . . There are no conditions of acceptance, no feeling of "I like you only if you are thus and so." (Rogers, 1957)

One of my students made the following observation in class: now that she has two small children she wants to 'go to all the parents I judged over the years and apologize for what I thought when their children were misbehaving in grocery stores'. Acceptance is not overlooking or even forgiving; it relates closely to empathy in that the rationale for acceptance is often based on understanding and fellow-feeling. The counsellor's job is to be so fully on each person's side that the common-sense judging of what are good and bad behaviours is naturally suspended in the focus on getting into the client's world. The counsellor is a passionate anthropologist going out to seek what there is to be learned.

A relational counsellor is often called upon to be non-judgemental in an atmosphere that is electrically charged with judgement. She may need a rationale for those who feel that her unwillingness to judge shows lack of caring, intelligence, courage or all three. (I once responded to demands for judgement and blame by an angry couple by saying that the fault lay entirely with their three-month-old baby!) One way to bypass judgement, internally as well as externally, has to do with responding to what the couples therapist Neal Jacobson has called the 'It' (Koerner and Jacobson, 1994: 220–22). The 'It' for him is the *shared situation* which is the context for struggles between persons. Couples and families often find themselves torn between blaming themselves or one another. They are freed from this dichotomy by acknowledgement that they are in a situation that was not caused by any one person's bad intentions. The counsellor is kept from judgement by focus on the simple fact that it is differing interpretations of reality that frustrate and keep people apart. For example, the counsellor might move from client to client to illustrate the way they share a common distress as well as very different ways of looking at it:

> Over here I'm a father who has got to tell my kid some important lessons and I'm real afraid of what will happen if my son doesn't learn them. Over here I'm thinking my father thinks I'm an idiot. He thinks I can't figure things out for myself.

Or to a husband who has withdrawn in the face of his wife's anger:

> Here is a husband who says, 'She's always so angry with me. All she wants to do anymore is get mad at me, tell me what I'm doing wrong. Anything I say just makes her madder. Why bother to even talk to her?' And here is his wife who says 'He really doesn't care how I feel. He doesn't want to listen to me. If he would listen even a little I wouldn't have to be so mad.'

The counsellor shows acceptance by a matter-of-fact demonstration of knowledge of what the family is up against. In the following brief example, both members of the couple were feeling consistently hurt and unsupported in the aftermath of change in their life that began with the birth of their first child:

Counsellor: You would really like some understanding from Jack. Jack how much understanding do you have for Cordelia right now?

Jack: I would have a lot if she wasn't always so critical of me. I will sympathize with her when she lets up on constantly, I mean constantly, telling me what's wrong with me.

Counsellor: You would have understanding for Cordelia, but you are unable to right now because you feel criticized so much by her. I'm getting two things then – that there may be some understanding there for her – but it's blocked because she is critical of you?

Cordelia: I don't *want* to be so critical. It just comes out of me . . . I feel so frustrated.

Counsellor: Can you picture that, Jack . . . that Cordelia would rather not be critical of you?

The counsellor is not just 'looking for the good' in the situation. He is *convinced* that people desire connection and relationship even while expressing distancing and judging positions as shown in Box 4.3. The counsellor can act to sort out the complexity of feelings that co-exist in the midst of accusatory, distancing language.

Box 4.3   Use of imagination to find unconditional positive regard

The counsellor may rely on her ability to connect with each individual's private reality to give empathy primacy over the urge to evaluate. Some situations, which vary for each counsellor, will challenge core values of the counselling. It may take use of imagination to find meaning in behaviour that is usually hard not to judge. In the following clinical example, the counsellor creates a little drama so that he can make a case for understanding a silent client's motivation:

A single mother has just lost her job. Her 13-year-old son has continued begging her to buy him tickets for a rock concert. The counsellor lines up three chairs and dramatizes three versions of what the boy is up to.

'Here are three boys whose mother has lost her job. The one in this chair is sorry for her – doesn't want to add to her worries. He understands that she's so worried about how to pay for food and housing that he would never think about disturbing her about a rock concert. "Oh mother," he says, "How can I help? Would you like me to sell my television?" This kid is nice to her. On the other hand, he might be doing

---

something that she doesn't want — getting so worried that he loses energy for his own sense of fun. What per cent of Peter is like this boy?' Mother and son laugh. The boy says 0 per cent. The mother says 30 per cent. In fact, some past sessions in counselling have been spent talking about Peter's sense of worry about his mother and there has been concern that he has over-identified with her dilemmas.

'The one in this chair says: "Mom, let me go to the concert. Please, please, let me go, please. Yeah I'm sorry about your job. Too bad — but please, please can I go to the concert? Just let me go, please." This kid doesn't seem to give a damn about what his mother is going through. On the other hand he really trusts his mother to take care of herself and to love him however he acts.' Mother and Peter laugh at this and Mother says: 'There has been quite a bit of that lately'. Peter says, 'That's the one. One hundred per cent.'

'The one in this last chair says: "Mom, I understand about your job loss and want to support you, but I want to keep my rights to be a kid. I want to trust you to figure out how to survive, and that includes saying no to me if you can't afford what I want. So I'm going to keep on being a kid, right now in my behaviour. I won't pretend to be any more mature than I am." This one sounds like a counsellor. Is there any of him?' Mother says: 'A bit, I think'. Peter gestures to indicate that there is some but not much.

The counsellor looks for language to find a perspective in a situation that could bring up either judgement (joining the mother in outrage at Peter's insensitivity and selfishness) or incongruence (portraying acceptance while feeling angry as Peter begged for the tickets and his mother, weary and discouraged, said no and tried to change the subject). The counsellor chose a humorous drama to place Peter's action in a developmental and fluid context and in doing so he also found a way to genuinely accept Peter as he was (and as OK), rather than ignore the situation.

Unconditional positive regard as awareness of intentions

The counsellor in relational counselling is aware always of hearing two messages: the first is the message of hurt or frustration which leads to anger and rejection; the other is the message of *wanting something different* – connection with the other or change in one's own life. In training programmes, I encourage role play in which counsellors in training facilitate disputes between two partners. Almost invariably the counsellor becomes exhausted by what amounts to a double bind with adversarial couples. He is torn between the equally inauthentic options of being a passive witness, theoretically acceptant of inauthentic ranting or of being a moralistic teacher ordering or pleading with people to behave better. A third choice is that of an active facilitator. In the following illustration, the counsellor is active not only in searching for the meaning which negative emotions have for each family member, but also is facilitating a dialogue that includes awareness of the effect of one person's emotions on the other.

> *Bob*: We are *NOT* asking my mother to call before she visits! I won't put her through that humiliation. If you loved me you would *never* ask me to humiliate my own 75-year-old mother.
>
> *Sue*: *Fine*! Let's have her move in completely. I'll make it easy for her. I'll move out. She can have them [the children] any time they are at your house. She just better stay the hell away from mine!
>
> *Counsellor*: Let me sort out what we have here so far. Bob, at this moment you feel as though Sue is asking you to seriously injure your mother by asking her to call. You feel that somehow Sue's request is an injury to you – a sign of her not loving you – so you are really angry! (Hold on, let me get this out and you both can comment on how close I come.) Sue, you feel backed into the corner by this. You feel so unheard that you would be willing to move out rather than fit in with Bob's expectations. You both feel forced into something that violates your core sense of what's right.

The counsellor's response might be understood in the following ways:

- as a reminder of the context of the couple not only talking with one another, but talking with one another in his presence: the counsellor needs to let himself be noticed when couples are caught in the spell of a defensive and accusatory mode;
- as a response to the underlying feelings that are driving the language: the counsellor is listening for what is urgent for Bob and Sue and is, as a by-product, down-playing both Bob's refusal to speak with his mother and Sue's threat to move out. The therapist would *not* screen out Bob telling Sue he will not ask something of his mother, or Sue telling Bob she wants to leave him and get her own place, if those statements were the heart of the communication.
- as recognition of a predicament which joins them both: communication of unconditional positive regard can be facilitated by acknowledgment of the power of the shared situation; the counsellor sees Bob and Sue as individuals, distinct not only from the complex situation with Bob's mother, but from the *unchosen frustrating style* that for now appears to be their only way to talk about it.

Box 4.4   A brief test of unconditional positive regard and multi-directional partiality

In couples counselling, the counsellor's gender may affect his or her immediate reaction to client words. What are your reactions to the following statements? How would these statements affect your sense of unconditional positive regard for the speaker? How would they affect your unconditional positive regard for the speaker's partner?

- 'I think he thinks it's his right to have sex with me. He's not medieval; he doesn't think I should do it every time he wants to, but he does think I should try to do it sometimes even if I don't feel like it. I don't think I should *ever* do it unless it's something I want to do for myself.'
- 'OK. He says, "Don't keep asking me about sex. Give me a chance to want it myself. Let me pursue you for a change." So I wait. It's been – what? – three or four weeks.'
- 'Look, I had an affair and I'm sorry. I've said I'm sorry about a hundred times. I've promised I won't do it again. What more do you want? How long do I have to expect you to be in a bad mood and wondering whether you are going to bring it up again?'
- 'I wish that just once I could come into the house and have you greet me without immediately telling me how late I am; how hard the kids have been; or demanding that I take over the kids, the dinner, my mother on the telephone or all three. Why can't you even be glad to see me? Ask how my day was?'
- 'I don't think you have any idea about what it takes to make this house run. You say you "*help out*" – that's it, you "*help out*". You help out, for a little while, when you feel like it, in a job that is really mine 24 hours a day, seven days a week.'
- 'I need one half day a week that is completely my own – no obligations to you or the kids; just mine to do what I want with. Is that too much to ask?'

Unconditional positive regard is shown according to the style of the counsellor

The counsellor's acceptance is shown in different ways by different counsellors. Not all successful relational counsellors are warm, although Rogers (1980: 19–22) makes a case for expression of appreciative feelings. Rather than warmth, some counsellors have the quality of seriousness and reserve which makes them a natural match for those families who are suspicious of what they see as easy kindness. Less expressive counsellors may relate to the family *beneath* surface impressions and give them reassurance non-verbally that they will each be taken seriously. Some other counsellors are naturally out-going. They pick up babies, delight in teenagers, feel the everyday drudgery of a working mother or father, laugh heartily at the family humour and are impressed by the regular achievements of growing children. In Chapter 5, I write at length about preparation for rela-tional counselling. It is the counsellor's task to focus both on her intention to receive clients unconditionally and the external cues within her style which might demonstrate that intention.

The counsellor experiences *empathy* for the clients' internal frame of reference

> To sense the client's private world as if it were your own, but without ever losing the "as if" quality – this is empathy. (Rogers, 1957)

The counsellor's realness and acceptance have no meaning outside the context of the quality that may perhaps be most characteristically person-centred, the capacity to empathize. Rogers (1980) called it 'an unappreciated way of being.' Empathy is the ability to be genuinely available to the moment's opportunity, to make enough room within oneself so that full understanding of some other person or thing may emerge rather than be forced. Carl Rogers was frustrated and turned off by any implication that this was a passive activity having to do with simply reflecting back what was said by the other (Kirschen-baum and Henderson, 1990: 127–28). For him, it was a large-hearted, generous venture that conveyed the force of the therapist's person-ality. Rogers was fond of quoting the ancient Chinese philosopher Lao Tsu and recalled these words with regard to empathy:

> It is as though he listened
> and such listening as his enfolds us in a silence
> in which at last we begin to hear
> what we are meant to be. (Rogers, 1980)

A person-centred counsellor has learned to focus on the under-standing of each client's personal meanings. Explicitly or implicitly the effective counsellor must always return to these questions: What do I know about what it is like for these clients? Am I getting it? Am I following them as they take their own direction?

Empathy and relational context

The practice of empathy for individual members of a family takes place in the context of empathy for the other family members who are also present. Timing matters and will be discussed in detail in chapters on beginning, middle and ending stages of therapy. Until a family or couple joins you or lets you join them, it is important to assume that your empathic listening for one family member can be understood by another as taking sides. Most of our clients do not come to us out of regular participation in person-centred group work! I seek permission and explicitly ask members for their capacity for silent observation:

> I'm going to be listening to dad's point of view for about five minutes. Will you be able to sit here during that time knowing that we are next going to be listening to what you want your dad to know about your point of view?

> I'm going to be over here joining in getting the female point of view on this issue. Don't worry that I'll forget that there is a male point of view that will then want to be heard. Actually you can worry all you want. I'm just saying, I'll be back to find out your take on all of this.

As counselling progresses clients often (but not always!) find themselves increasingly comfortable with the give and take of the multi-person session and more secure that there will be room for them to be heard: 'Go ahead. Hear him out. Just don't forget to give me a turn.'

Empathy and family members who are silent

Empathy in family therapy is as much for the listeners as it is for the speakers. In the following counselling session the counsellor responds to what he feels it must be like for a silent member of a family:

> In therapy with a family of adolescents and a mother, the topic gets around to 'What's wrong with Doug?' Doug's mother is discouraged. There is bad news from school; he is failing in three subjects and getting thrown out of class for talking too much. His older brother weighs in with comments: 'He's a jerk. He isn't doing anything right.' There is a flood of criticism. Doug shrinks on the couch. The counsellor says to himself 'OOPS, this isn't what they have come for!' He stands up. (Sometimes with a family which has become trapped into a discouraging attack mode – especially toward a child or teen – I stand up without exactly knowing what I will do next.)

'Doug, can we switch places here for a moment? Thanks.' The counsellor gets in Doug's chair: 'I'm the youngest,' he says, 'Everybody is my boss. Everybody can tell me what to do. Everybody can tell me I'm the family screw up. I *am* the family screw up. But they can't make me do better in school if I don't want to. They can't make me! How close is that to it for you, Doug?'

'Pretty close.'

In this example the counsellor saw that a family pattern had been activated. A wave of criticism and worry washed over the identified patient who withdrew, feeling judged and not able to have a voice except by acting out. The counsellor's task was to be present to Doug's 'private world' as well as to that of his family. The counsellor chose not to attempt to draw out the client in the presence of his older brother. In the past, that resulted in increased acting out or sullen withdrawal by both of them. In later sessions, Doug would find his own voice and not need such an active counsellor.

Empathy and respect for the family culture

Clients come in with a common culture, complex family structure and hierarchy; and the counsellor's role is facilitation, not correction. When a counsellor listens respectfully to the opinion of a 14-year-old about the foolishness of punishing teenagers for physical fights with their teachers, he is not facilitating a parliamentary debate about a new policy, he is allowing everyone's voice to be heard in a respectful context. Following Milton Erickson, psychiatrist and inspiration for *Uncommon Therapy* (Haley, 1973), the counsellor, in this example, makes room for both person and hierarchical role:

'I want you, Dad, to sit in the father's chair and give the father's opinion while I sit here with Jack, knowing that he may disagree with everything his father says . . .'

[Or, to the teenager] 'Let's sit here in the teenager's section and talk about how we see things that the adults don't understand.'

By means of play, the relational counsellor facilitates contact between people, which makes their relationships more complex and rich. He allows them to express strong opinions without getting locked in a battle for prevalence. In so doing he does not set the therapy up against the outer world where people function in roles and with structure. 'Don't forget folks,' the sage Carl Whitaker admonished a group of therapists in a 1990 San Diego conference, 'What happens in here [the therapy room] is pretend. They have to go out to their own real world.'

Empathy and identification

Meeting a family group or a couple stirs the emotions. The wise counsellor is not someone who has achieved a sense of balance, but one who knows how easily he can be unbalanced. Person-centred family therapist Ned Gaylin emphasizes the distinction between empathy and identification: '. . . a person who is identified with another does not maintain any distance . . . identification is more dangerous to the therapeutic process because it permits the therapist to project motivations onto the client that are outside the client's frame of reference' (Gaylin, 1989: 273). Becoming identified with one member of a couple or family can interfere with effective counselling even more than identification in individual counselling, because it can create a temporary alignment with one person's interests and a lack of empathy for her opponent. One way for the counsellor to guard against this is to invite comment on the effects of his words; for example:

> How am I doing on fairness here? I *think* I'm helping Maria lay out her position. Am I sounding like I've joined the Maria team?

Clients are at least to a minimum degree able to perceive these qualities

> The final condition as stated is that the client perceives, to a minimal degree, the acceptance and empathy that the therapist experiences for him. Unless some communication of these attitudes has been achieved, then such attitudes do not exist in the relationship as far as the client is concerned, and the therapeutic process could not by our hypothesis, be initiated. (Rogers, 1957)

Ned Gaylin comments on Rogers' sixth condition:

> Here, finally, the family therapist may have it easier than the therapist working with individuals. In so far as the condition indicates at least a minimal perception by the client(s), it may be sufficient if at certain times only some members perceive the therapist as caring and understanding. (Gaylin, 1989: 275)

The therapist is not there to please all the people all the time and will lose the core conditions if she attempts to do so. Family members act out – at home and in family therapy. That is, they go into various states of non-cooperation or over-cooperation. Feeling safe, they sometimes experiment with extremes of behaviour, including feeling excluded and sided-against by the therapist. The counsellor uses supervision, reflection and team processing between the sessions to learn whether she is doing what she can to be ready for the meeting. Frequently there is some empathic response that will emerge with attention; or some unspoken genuine reaction which would be facilitative; or some judgement that needs to be worked through in order to be truly available to one or another client. Sometimes, however, the counsellor may not feel able to be useful to someone who will later turn out to have benefited greatly from a process that permitted his mother, sister, partner or child to find his or her voice.

The medium of family therapy involves active communication with a diverse group. Therapeutic conditions are best communicated by a person who is sensitive to the meaning clients may place upon her words and actions. Family therapy literature over the last 15 years has emphasized the need to tune into the culture of the families we meet so that we can adjust our communication to their world view. On a broader scale, works like *Ethnicity and Family Therapy* (McGoldrick et al., 1982) have shown ways in which family therapists show respect for the customs and language of each ethnic group. In microcosm, however, all families and all individuals have their own ways of interpreting a counsellor's behaviour. Her effectiveness depends on her ability to translate her intentions and responses into language that makes sense to them. Box 4.5 illustrates one attempt to facilitate more than one person's experience of the core conditions.

Box 4.5 Looking for the path to respect for everyone

In a session with a single mother and her three teenage boys, the oldest boy (16) took a seat in the centre of the room and with everybody's consent (for a while) held forth with a barrage of complaints about his life. As his complaining grew in volume and he became more and more definite about negative opinions about every aspect of his life, I could see that his mother was getting more and more uncomfortable. When he told a story in which he called someone an obscene name, she was definitely embarrassed and said sarcastically, 'What wonderful language I've taught you'. At that point I gradually interrupted the oldest boy with questions about whether or not he would be able to handle his mother joining the conversation with her response to what he had to say. With his consent, I then asked his mother if she would be willing to take the chair her son was in (which I had labelled now the speaker's chair) and talk about her thoughts about his angry words. I asked him to sit where his mother was sitting and just listen. When his mother took the chair, she expressed some of her own opinions about the family life and what her son had been saying. He was able to listen as she spoke; and later, with nobody in the speaker's chair, they had an exchange about a variety of issues in which they both were engaged and in contact.

In a training programme discussion of a video of this session, I was asked why I had asked the mother and son to change chairs. My first response was that I just couldn't stand his going on any longer with his mother and brothers treated as invisible. My second was simply that I had wanted to give the mother a chance to have a voice in the presence of this dominating oldest son who appeared not to be able to listen. One of my listeners, an experienced person-centred counsellor, gave the best expression of my intention: '*You did it out of respect for her*'. I could not show respect for her without responding in some way to her diminishment as his words went on and on. I also wanted to show respect for her son by asking for a way for him to allow his mother to enter the conversation without implying a criticism of his style of talking or his having said so much about himself. If I had simply made a process comment – 'You are doing all the talking while your mother shows discomfort and tries unsuccessfully to speak' – he would have taken that as a criticism by an adult and would have been shut down.

CHAPTER 5

Preparation for Relational Therapy

Sometimes while a family or couple waited at the San Diego Family Institute, I used to walk around a long, narrow circular corridor in our back building where my office was located. I was getting ready to see them and out-walking my fear of displeasing, my need to have some solution to their problem that didn't involve their skill or effort, my sense of self-righteous indignation at one member or my urgent protectiveness of another. I was walking to get my feet on the ground and my breathing regular so that I would not get swept away into pretending I was a member of the family. At times I would have to pace for a long time to out-walk an urgency to join parents in criticism and worry about their teenagers or to join one parent and his or her children against another. Now, somewhat more experienced and without those corridors, I often sit in my chair and look at the chairs of all the people on their way or waiting outside my door. I am looking to remember that I am able to sit in my own chair, breathe for myself and do my best; and that I am here to facilitate their doing the same.

Sometimes I remember that children are coming and need to check that I have toys appropriate for their age and that my crayons and magic markers are in order. More than one smaller adult client has needed me to remember to bring in a chair from the waiting room that allowed her feet to touch the ground. For some clients a dish of candy is appreciated and becomes a ritual. For other clients, candy should be eliminated – and not just for hyperactive children and diabetics. One wife (and I!) used to get hypnotized into a critical mood by watching her husband's step by step demolition of all the candy in my office. For supervision or training I sometimes need to set up video or audio equipment.

Once I realized that a family with a teenage girl was on the way and that she was about to go as usual to sit on my huge reclining chair designated for individual clients, while her parents and I sat on the simpler matching chairs meant for meetings with families. Her sitting on that chair above and apart from the frustrated rest of us seemed a symbol of her attempts to get comfortable while evoking the disapproval which was the great discomfort of her life. We were about to start the session annoyed with her while prevented by the rules of permissive therapist etiquette from commenting on it. I quickly piled two other chairs on top of the large chair and added a sign saying 'off limits'. This preparation set the stage for my meeting her with a lively humorous stand about what I could and could not do in my own office and freed me from the stiff, covertly disliking posture I was in with her. She joined in the spirited argument with me after a race in which I protected *my* usual chair; and the laughing we all did led to more genuine conversation about the family predicament.

Every therapist prepares for any therapy, including relational therapy. When a family or couple comes in I am in some state of readiness for them that can range from openness and curiosity to fear and dislike to embarrassed defensiveness because the space is not ready for them. The question is *how* do I prepare? Being a busy person who goes from one client group to the next without reflection or recovery is a version of preparation. You want to do your best. But which you? Which best? Who will show up as counsellor? I hope someone who is neither a nice guy sitting in, trying without scolding to get everyone to improve their behaviour, nor an elegant showman telling people how to be a couple, parents or children. Someone who, I hope, is *mindful*, as family therapist David Sanders (1997) describes the goal of his brief preparation for therapy.

Asked about his own preparation for relational therapy, Sanders talks about: 'Little insignificant things, like making sure the room is ready and that there are enough chairs.' He describes: '. . . how you arrange the office and wondering who is going to sit where. Then taking a few moments to think: "Where were we last time?"' Before the session, preparation may mean looking at videotapes, listening to audio tapes, consulting another counsellor and awareness such as 'I was too hard on this mother whom I really don't understand' or 'I don't think I connected with the father in this family'.

The check-in may take the form of awareness of one's own defensiveness, fear or the need to control that both pre-exists any family you might meet and can be stimulated by the meeting with any actual family. For preparation for a family one has never met before, David Sanders paraphrases an old supervisor, 'Don't worry if you don't know what you're doing; the patient will help you! . . . this is more true the more people you are seeing. A facilitative remark is more likely to be helpful, the more people there are to hear it.'

Carl Rogers' preparation for therapy with individuals was to ask for a few moments in which, as he said, he would take time out to focus his attention on the moment and the client before him. He would then come out of what seemed to be a meditation and turn to the client and say something like: 'I am available to be here with you for this period of time for whatever you would like to do' (1979). Although his immediate preparation was brief and uncomplicated, his long-term preparation was reflective, self-challenging and open to paradox. In his autobiography (1967) Rogers talked about the decades in which he was fortunate enough to spend 20 hours a week seeing clients. Each of those hours was accompanied by at least one other hour of reflection, dialogue, research, writing and listening to client tapes. The Carl Rogers who attended to clients' cognition and emotions with such intellectual and emotional availability was formed by the moments spent outside of therapy. Just as our clients' lives are formed by what happens before and between therapy sessions, so our readiness to be useful is formed by what we think and do about what we are in our counselling.

In his article 'Characteristics of a Helping Relationship', Rogers asks ten questions which may be seen as the setting of the stage for a meeting before it occurs (1961d). For example, he asks 'Can I be in some way which will be perceived by the other person as trustworthy, as dependable or consistent in some very deep sense?' and 'Can I be expressive enough as a person so that what I am will be communicated unambiguously?' The reader and any counsellor would do well to read those questions (1961d: 50–55). The following sections deal with five questions I may ask which relate directly to relational therapy.

Can I be hopeful in a way that is drawn from observation and true experience rather than from wishful thinking or dutiful cheerfulness?

In both 'Solution Oriented Therapy' (de Shazer, 1985) and 'Narrative Therapy' (White and Epston, 1990) emphasis is placed on questions which gather information about unnoticed family success, acts of kindness, signs of courage, dignity and reflectiveness. 'Family therapy has always emphasized what clients can do rather than focusing on what they can't do well' (Taffel, 1995). The counsellor manages to orient herself toward acknowledgement of what, unnoticed, is a sign of hopefulness.

The counsellor does not gather this sense of the positive from thin air or by his own unquenchable optimism (my own natural optimism has been tested as below average (Seligman, 1990) and has never even approached unquenchable!). Before he begins a session in which problems and discouragement and mutual contempt may predominate, he needs to be mindful of data that are encouraging. Can I derive confidence from the fact that everyone individually has made this journey to be together in my office and know that initiating energy existed before the meeting with me and will continue after it? American humorist Woody Allen has said: 'Eighty per cent of life is just showing up'. In some of the apparently chaotic families which seek or are sent for counselling, it seems a miracle that such unco-operative, alienated people could be assembled in the room. I reflect on this, pacing or sitting in a trance in my chair. It is *not* a miracle. It is *the formative tendency* at work before the session even starts. The simple attendance by the most alienated teenager or distancing husband is behaviour that can be more significant than any seeming lack of cooperation or participation.

Sometimes, between sessions, I write letters to clients (see White and Epston, 1990, and Epston, 1994, for good examples of letters to clients). Mine usually begin: 'Why are you here? . . .' because in the answer to that question is the open door to the clients' own hope, wishes and intentions. Some of the letters I rewrite to be given or read to clients; most simply serve the purpose of counsellor mind-fulness. I have also written letters that begin: 'I think we should cancel this session . . .' and continue until something emerges from my picture of the clients and who they can be which contradicts my own activated fears or pessimism.

I frequently remind myself and sometimes announce to a family that I assume that 90 per cent of what they have been doing has worked very well and that we are working on the 10 per cent which they want to re-examine. This cute phrase can be comforting for me. More comforting by far is awareness of the successful facts of a family's life. Why *have* these kids gone to school and been successful in school, all these mornings over all these years? Why *can* this mother who fears they will fight angrily tonight know, without having to focus on it, that they will get themselves up to appear in school with their homework done tomorrow morning?

Once, after a convoluted discussion about how to handle a large family gathering involving three generations of several families, my sister-in-law suddenly said, 'Let's pretend that everybody's normal for a few minutes!' Acting as if people didn't need to be managed or directed into some formula gives room for individual initiative and counts on a human adaptability which, if it exists, gives life its richness and if it doesn't exist, certainly makes counselling a hopeless enterprise. The counsellor acts as if everybody's voice if heard will lead not to a neatly packaged resolution, but to a state in which trust in family members' ability to handle social complexity becomes heightened by acceptance and respect.

Can I care about this family or couple while at the same time remaining separate and allowing them to be responsible for their life?

Am I strong enough in my separateness that I will not be downcast in his depression, frightened by his fear, nor engulfed by his dependency? Is my inner self hardy enough to realize that I am not destroyed by his anger, taken over by his need for dependence, nor enslaved by his love, but that I exist separately with feelings and rights of my own? (Rogers, 1961d: 52)

In relational therapy, says Breffni Barrett, 'You need confidence and trust in the process. Don't take too much responsibility. People are entitled to their suffering. It confuses people when you are too attached to an outcome.'

Family therapist Peggy Papp has talked in workshops about a tool she uses in supervision called *'bad therapy'*. In order to relieve trainee anxiety and fear of 'failing miserably', Ms Papp sometimes asks 'who will volunteer to go in and do bad therapy?'. 'It gives people permission to make mistakes' (Papp, 1998). In an exercise I have derived from this idea, the counsellor, in the presence of supportive colleagues or a supervisor, role-plays saying or doing whatever she might feel like saying or doing with clients but feels prevented by decorum, human decency, professional ethics or the law of the land. In such role plays, self-consciousness, the desire to portray a certain quality, brittle propriety, pretence and tension give way to energy and, frequently, to awareness of the counsellor's truest responses and deepest intentions. Sometimes, of course, the counsellor locates fears, judgements, identification and projection that belonged to his life long before his clients and need expression entirely outside of counselling. On other occasions the now less inhibited counsellor discovers something that she truly does want to say that is a congruent reaction in a dynamic relationship. It can also happen that the counsellor discovers a more compassionate understanding of a person's situation that is free to be configured only after she is relieved of the job of trying not to judge. Naturally, counselling improves when a counsellor's covert attempts to control and reform are exposed and can be released.

Of course, one good supervisor, listening well, can bring about the same effects in helping the counsellor to hear herself, her own fears, urgencies, prejudices, wishes and disappointments. However it happens, the counsellor's task is to separate out her own self from that of the clients. Clients' anger, incongruence, discouragement or defensiveness become part of the material of counselling rather than the counsellor's personal problem.

Can I find a way to be on the side of each member of the family?

While remaining free to express my own opinions, values and feelings, can I relate to each person as an individual with her own legitimate perspective and entitlement to a hearing? Can I sort out what members of the family have made me afraid, defensive, self-righteous or urgently crusading? Can I sort out which members have made me protective, reverent, or driven to heroic advocacy? Can I be continually curious about my very human tendency to align myself with or against this or that person?

In supervision about relational therapy that seems to be going badly, a counsellor will frequently talk of his frustration with a couple and family, and present one person who does not seem to be his client as much as his adversary. For example:

> In a case conference about a couple, I found myself playing the role of the husband; and I became aware how definitely the counsellor saw him as an obstacle to the counselling rather than as her client. Without noticing it, the counsellor had perceived the wife as a person in need and the husband as a person who was withholding the caring and support which was needed. The more she talked of his lack of participation in the counselling, the more, in the role of husband, I told of my own frustration and disappointment in my wife's increasing depression. The more the counsellor seemed to be explaining how I could be more helpful to my wife, the more I expressed the frustration at having my own point of view ignored. 'Perhaps you are wanting to be my client, too?' said the counsellor, with good-natured irony as she realized that the husband would not change without attention as an individual with needs of his own.

Can I be congruent, clear and in control of my role in sessions so that clients feel safe, respected and uncoerced by one another?

It is important to be strong in relation to those aspects of the counselling that pertain to us, our offices and the contract of the counselling rather than in relation to choices and a way of being which pertain to the client. We do not get in the way of our clients, nor do we stand by indiscriminately while they get in each other's way. A good facilitator is aware of the never-quite-arrived-at state of the right amount of chaos. If there is too much chaos, anxiety can go out of control and symptoms can erupt, with people becoming unable to tolerate a session of relational counselling. If, however, there is an attempt to suppress chaos rather than to find the meanings and intentions within a situation, it is not the person-centred approach.

I prepare myself to facilitate dialogue and am therefore prepared, for example, to assist a person with a dominating style to say what is important without blocking another's opportunity to do likewise. In an interview (see Chapter 10), a young client says that relational counselling is different 'because at home . . . *you are kind of putting your feelings onto somebody*, whereas here it's more open'. I prepare to offer habitually passive listeners an opportunity to respond to rather than endure another's words. Likewise I work with persons who are hard-to-interrupt talkers in order to make possible the difficult (for them) task of listening.

'You need a strong personality', says Breffni Barrett, who has one, 'Being timid and meek is a liability.' If, however, like me, you have to deal with timidity or meekness or a habit of self-doubt, preparation and supervision can focus you on the heart of counselling. Talking through the situation with a colleague can clarify our role. For example, how can a counsellor prepare to encounter an authoritarian man with a loud voice? I do not want to scold him into sullen silence; nor take on responsibility for teaching him better manners. I simply want him, for the length of the sessions, to speak in paragraphs rather than chapters so that other people may have their turn as well. I sometimes have to interrupt and be assertive to make this possible. The more I am prepared with accurate empathy for his predicament and his aspirations, the less defensive he will be. Paradoxically, his experience of me as on his side, unconditionally, allows him to accept my equal concern for his significant others.

I prepare for counselling by reflecting on the clients' stated wishes about the counselling – usually to get out of a frustrating cycle of mutual disrespect and to get closer to a state of empathic genuine support. The counsellor can model respect for herself as well as other qualities. She does not have to let herself in for an impossible situation or be part of an enterprise for which she cannot have respect. If someone comes to give an extensive accusatory speech, to not allow another to speak, or to insult his significant others, then the counsellor is prepared to engage him about his congruence with the purpose of the meetings. Unconditional positive regard for clients does not mean that a meeting is without conditions.

Carl Rogers was unconditionally acceptant, but never weak or unconscious of his own importance and rights. For example, those who watched him in demonstrations would notice how absolutely precise he was about ending the session at the agreed-upon time no matter how emotionally intense the counselling moment was.

If a client expects me to join them in persuading or manipulating another client to change, I need to clarify my intentions. It is not useful for a counsellor to be used even for a benevolent purpose. Box 5.1 illustrates the kind of clarification that can be required before counselling begins.

Box 5.1 Sometimes preparation means letting go of expectations that third parties may place upon the counselling

A long message on my voicemail from a referral source urges me to do something! My colleague is the individual counsellor of the mother of a family with three teenage boys who come to me for family therapy. The mother feels out of control of the behaviour of the youngest. My colleague reflects the mother's distress and confusion and urges me to do something about it in the family session planned for tonight. 'Can you use some of the session time to teach the mother how to apply negative consequences tonight? She needs help, is feeling out of control and needs you to do something.'

I really needed my preparation time to let go of that colleague's urgent voice and the voice in my own head that did think I should try to do as she asked. The knowledge that a family is in fear and chaos invites professionals to attempt to *seem* helpful at the expense of the confident imaginative responses that can actually be of use. I am in support of a mother being able to respond to the abusive actions of any children in a family. I am also committed to the family counselling as a place where everyone gets heard and everyone gets a chance to work on the problems they share in common. I would not enter the session with a teaching or parenting agenda, but would remember my purpose of giving each person, including the mother and including the youngest son, a voice and a chance at the counselling meeting.

I had one of my best sessions with this struggling family. As a matter of fact, I was able to confirm the mother's desire for more limits and for her voice to be stronger in the family. Before that, however, I was able to be a voice for the youngest child's sense of hurt, sense of grievance and unfairness. And before any of that, I had to enter the session as a person interested in every sovereign individual entering the room, not as the mother's partner.

Can I be aware of my own vulnerability to client incongruence, whether shown by anger, dependence, manipulation or withholding?

Preparation for family counselling means shedding our projections in order to widen our view of a whole person communicating. Some clients are angry, withholding, seemingly disdainful of counselling, silent, or possibly in some way like a counsellor's own father, mother, sister or brother. A counsellor needs preparation to see the unspoken other half of a client's communication: the hurt or longing contained in the anger; the fear behind the witholding; and the discouragement that disdain can sometimes signify (see Mearns, 1994a, about the unspoken relationship). Preparation for counselling means that we work out our dislike of a client rather than take that out on our client. The counsellor needs to remind herself that client incongruence is the heart of the work at hand, not an obstacle or a sign of the counsellor's inadequacy. 'The clients are right on schedule' [with whatever form their incongruence may take] is a favourite phrase of one experienced supervisor.

If a counsellor is able to shed her sense of defensiveness about one client's authoritarian blustering she may connect with him by understanding his sense of not belonging and his wish to be included. I once had a client say that the moment when she was at her most angry and most insulting to her husband was also exactly the time she was most fearful of being abandoned and unloved. Box 5.2 closes the chapter with an ongoing struggle to relate to other dimensions of frustrating client behaviour.

Box 5.2 Why can't clients behave as I want them to?

I would be an excellent counsellor if only my clients didn't insist on doing the following things and more:

1. *Accuse each other in insulting, unequivocal language.* Can I ask myself and sometimes them about what hurt they most want their partner to know about? Can I ask them about what response they were hoping for?

2. *Sit silently smouldering and resist invitations to join in – then later say that the session was a waste of time or just there to attack them.* Can I reach out to them early enough in the session so that they know that I take them seriously and want the counselling to be directed by all the clients present? Can I invite comment on the process itself as an early legitimate part of our work? Can I check out impressions that they are uncomfortable in a way that is matter-of-fact and not threatening?

3. *Make threats or demands they don't mean and, having made them, try to be consistent with them.* Can I listen to the intentions and hopes that are expressed in the threats and demands? Can I notice when the same client says something softer and less threatening?

4. *Make a long speech about the faults of a teenager or child as though their thoroughness of accusation will somehow win over the sullen defiant young person in front of them.* Can I be flexible and strong

enough to facilitate a conversation which places the negative in a context?

5. *Speak in a self-absorbed, regressed way that makes her partner and the counsellor wonder if she were aware that others were in the room listening.* Can I be respectful of individual ways of expression and unique responses to the emotional impact of a couples or family meeting? Can I be flexible in interchanging individual and couple or family counselling as we try to arrive at a contract that makes sense to all involved?

6. *Get so angry that they can't behave with even minimal courtesy to one another.* Can I accept their right to feel and show anger while I hold them accountable for their agreement to attempt a dialogue? Can I be creative both in accepting anger and in tracking its meaning in the dialogue of the counselling?

CHAPTER 6

Getting Started

As a client in relational counselling, I have been the subject of more than one first session. One was positive: the therapist loved my oldest daughter, had connected with her over time in individual therapy and was able as well to relate to my wife and me. She listened to herself for a felt sense of what was going on in our family as well as listening to our words. She knew what it was like for teenage girls with developmental disabilities as well as for their parents. She also was able to know the four members of our family as persons distinct from the categories of age, profession and life challenges. Her first session was based on the needs of our daughter; emphasized the positive; encouraged the emergence of the younger person's voice; and kept her parents' always ready worries and speeches in the background. Her approach was similar to the work of person-centred counsellor Ned Gaylin who sometimes seeks pre-first session under-standing from parents that he will go out of his way to create a positive atmosphere for children and teenagers without taking their side against their parents (Gaylin, 1993).

Another very different first session with a therapist who had been highly recommended to us as experienced in working with families, led me to fantasize congratulations to the therapist for having the courage to give so little of herself; to have not even faked caring or having something to give! She had no words of delight about my talkative and warm daughter; no concern about my rushed and stressed wife; nor any curiosity about why we had chosen to drive across the city to see her rather than a counsellor closer to our home. She may have helped me unintentionally by reminding me of how even a generous and intelligent person can get lost behind paperwork obligations and the routine of one's work. There may have been a person there who would have become involved in our family predicaments with us. Unable to find the slightest reason for ever driving to her distant office again, we never found out.

Another counsellor to whom we, in fact, committed (after a lot of asking and searching in our new city) was warm and caring but at first busy with technique and too deferential to the parents in our family. She asked us several formula *solution-oriented* questions (Berg and Miller, 1992) that we had to politely sit through while we said in effect: 'Yes, yes, but I really had hoped we could talk about this great frustration we have been having . . .' and then later: 'But you know I think Martha and I could talk your ear off, but we really need you to be sure to give Gwen (our 18-year-old daughter) more of a chance to get this counselling to be her way'. Something about the counsellor, however, (her acceptance of us, and her genuine willingness to empathize?) made us willing to stop looking for someone else. Even though I had had exactly 20 years more experience in family counselling than our counsellor, her sheer goodwill, understanding of Gwen's special needs, willingness to hear us all, and her lack of defensiveness when we told her that we want more of this or less of that made our meetings important, helpful occasions.

Experiencing what it is like to be a client in relational therapy has sharpened my awareness of how I want to be in the beginning sessions of my own work as counsellor. This chapter is devoted to my own developing sense of counsellor tasks in beginning sessions of relational counselling.

Welcome each client

First and most important, I must welcome everyone into the session with acceptance and individual attention. This is most clear for me when children come. If they are younger than 10 or 11, I am a part of the adult world *who is either glad to see them and very interested in them or who prefers to remain detached as another adult whose business is with other grown-ups*. I have to find out what they do; where they go to school and what they know about the counselling. I am interested in who is the most talkative; who is the silliest; who is an artist; who plays sports; and who gets along with whom. I find out how long they think they can talk; how long they can listen to their parents talk; and if they know where the bathroom is. I offer them drawing materials and sometimes toys. They are given a place to sit in on the conversation and a place to get away from the centre of things and just listen in. I joke and make obvious mistakes about their ages, interests and other things. I have come to think of it as borderline malpractice not to have some small gift for children under the age of seven to take away with them. All of these things come out of me quite naturally when I realize that unless they feel like welcomed guests, the office will be forever a place where grown-ups make them come.

Teenagers and pre-teens are another matter, in that *respect* for them is paramount; and warm greetings, questions and joking are all secondary to responding to their level of receptivity. Many times they come after some trouble has happened and are eager to have me facilitate a conversation with their parents. On other occasions I simply acknowledge their desire to be silent without making a big deal about it. Often a simple respectful explanation about what I see as the purpose of the meeting will suffice as long as it includes room for them to talk or not to talk. Sometimes throwing a volleyball around the room is a way to make contact with those for whom physical activity is natural and intense verbal engagement is foreign. A teenager may be brought alone by his or her mother (or, less frequently, father) and I find it important to give him or her the priority in choosing whether we stay together or whether I meet first with the parent and then with him or vice versa.

Perhaps, the unique challenge of relational counselling becomes most clear in working together with teens and their parents. How can I facilitate a conversation between people who are usually highly sensitive to each other's judgements even while they feel free to speak angrily and critically? How can I be present as a non-judgemental individual in an atmosphere in which all the parties feel very exposed and judged? In individual work, the counsellor creates safety and acceptance by not interrupting and not trying to control the direction or pace of clients' expression. In relational work, the counsellor is active in co-creating a setting for a safe conversation for more than one person. She may interrupt; she may set the pace and she may need to be sensitive to one or more clients being driven away by a seemingly humiliating environment. If safety is created in early sessions, each person in a couple or family will not only find their voice but find a way to listen to the other without feeling judged.

I am always careful to get involved so that a potentially long monologue by the parent is postponed in favour of the beginnings of dialogue. For example:

> *Mother*: Billy has been in trouble in school. He was doing very well until he was about 12, then he changed. Now he doesn't care about anything but his friends and doing what he feels like. I try everything and nothing does any good. He just doesn't care.
>
> *Counsellor*: Sounds like you are very concerned about what is happening with Billy. Let me get Billy into this conversation. How would you describe what is happening, Billy?

Billy may be willing and able to talk about the situation. If, however, he seems to be perceiving the conversation as a discussion of his crimes and misdemeanours *between two adults*, I need temporarily to change the subject. I may back up a bit and talk about other things the family might want me to know about them. I may gently ask questions until I have an indication that we are on a subject that engages the young person. I may set up a *parents' chair* in which everyone may take turns sitting and saying what the parent thinks is wrong with the family, and what the parent thinks is good with the family. Box 6.1 contains reflections on contact with people who may benefit most from respectful family counselling.

Box 6.1 Talking with teenagers

Many counsellors disqualify themselves by saying they cannot connect with adolescents and thus join the majority of adults who leave older children lonely and dependent only on each other for dialogue and recognition. Others, seeing teenagers as some exotic different breed, adopt an artificially confident and confiding style with them. My own counselling with teenagers changes significantly when I remember that the most distant and/or disdainful young person has a story to tell. I am interested in what kids want, think about, fear, enjoy and hope. I find that if I am curious about many things in a respectful way, then young clients will satisfy the curiosity that is at the heart of counselling: what are their feelings about the most important issues in their lives?

Listed below are some of the forms of statements and questions I ask teenagers who have not yet found a way to be engaged in counselling (once they are engaged, I often need only to facilitate some kind of fair order so that everyone has a chance to speak). My words attempt to convey my interest and set the stage for connection. Until a teenager finds his voice I feel I have to give in order to receive. The only difference between an effective counsellor and an intruder is that the former is, first, genuinely interested in the answers to his questions and, second, will stop asking questions once there is an easy flow of client conversation. I may say:

- I am just very interested in whatever you want to say about what's important to you in all this.
- (To teenagers alone) I have worked it out with your parent(s) that everything you tell me in private is confidential. I need to know whether or not you are convinced that I mean that and will abide by it. I think you can see how important this will be if this counselling is to be useful.
- What part of this issue do you think we are overlooking?
- When your parents say, 'Just go back to school!' what is it that they may not understand that would make that difficult for you at this time?
- What do you think is happening now for kids who are 14 that is different from when your parents were 14?

- What are the conditions under which kids *want* parents and other adults in their lives and when do kids want parents to keep their distance?
- What areas of family life still involve you and what are parts of family life about which you wish they would leave you alone?
- What part of this (whatever their parents have presented as the problem) have you been thinking about?
- In what way should your parent(s) understand that your family life is different from your (older/younger) (brother/sister)?
- (To a 15-year-old) What are some of the things that have changed with you since you were 13? If I came to your school what would I see the 13-year-olds doing that I wouldn't see the 15-year-olds doing?
- What per cent of your life do your parents understand? What per cent do they not understand? What is something you would most like them to understand better?
- Who at your school do you consider a really successful kid? Who do you and others you know admire and think does well at life?

The specific questions are not as important as the *attitude* they convey: that I don't claim to know the experience of teenagers and would like to know more. What are your preferred ways of talking with teenagers? What may keep you from connecting with the teenagers who, with or without their families, might become your clients? Can you enlist them as experts who will help you?

Still another matter is welcoming the adult who is most reluctant to be present. In couples counselling it is important that the least willing member be given maximum chance to join the conversation. The counsellor may ask, 'What brought you here today?' followed by questions that provide guidance about how to get into the conversation and reassurance that his language and way of doing things are just as acceptable as that of his more comfortable partner. Some such questions are:

- If this counselling were really helpful for you John, what would happen differently at home?
- If you had initiated this counselling what would we be talking about?
- Phil, its your turn. You can talk about this topic that Angela has brought up or you can bring up anything that you like, whether it fits in with what she said or not.
- What do you think we should know about you, Maria? What would you like us to know about you? (Anderson, 1997)

With some couples and families, it becomes important to give each person some time alone with the counsellor. For others, it would be an interruption to separate the couple or family group. These people are able to be safe in conversation and are trying to go forward in it. When couples are so hostile that they can barely allow the other to speak, I ask for time alone with each of them. In addition to connecting with them and being able to listen to them without needing to protect another family member, I also challenge them with the problem of how they will handle my relating with equal respect to their partner.

Find out why everyone has come

In beginning work with couples, person-centred counsellor Elke Lambers says: 'I probably talk more. I have to keep everyone's attention. As therapy goes on, I become quieter.' She is conscious that in individual therapy you can take for granted each person's willingness to be there, but in relational therapy, one person has usually been asked or pressured to come and may initially feel little openness to invest herself.

She spends time asking questions about why they are here and how they feel. Elke also spends time with ground-rules and 'what my place is in the whole'. She explains so that they will understand that the focus will be kept on them and their important conversation is with each other. Elke also lets people know that 'this can be a difficult and at times unpleasant experience'. She lets them know that she will not be upset by it. Elke tells people that this is their relationship and that they know more about it than she ever can.

Norm Chambers, a student and colleague of Rogers' for 20 years and a trainer and teacher from the person-centred approach for over 30 years, describes himself as 'in a learning mode' in first session. He frequently asks himself the question 'how come they are here?' He sometimes follows a family in whatever direction they take and sometimes stops action to ask 'what's going on here?' On his mind is 'what's not working for them – that's what brought them here'. Similar to the *solution-oriented therapists* (Berg and Miller, 1992) he is curious about what things would look like if the therapy were helpful. Chambers describes his sense of the person-centred approach in this way: 'I'm very hopeful that what people want – as they define it – is achievable. Actually it is not a hope. It is based on a lot of experience: what I believe about humans. People always want to be better than what they are – as they define it.'

The question 'What brought you in here?' and variations such as 'Are you here for the same reason that Gail is here?', or 'Are we talking about what you wanted to talk about?' are important ways to make contact with all the clients. In relational counselling, there are always multiple interests and preferred ways to approach a common topic. The counsellor, in experimenting with different questions, encourages the perception that there are many ways of entering the family or couple conversation. I have found that counsellor silence in early sessions tends to encourage only those clients who already understand how counselling can be useful for them. It can be helpful to facilitate expression of client expectations and to make explicit my own expectations in order deal with assumptions such as those detailed in Box 6.2.

Box 6.2   Clients may be following rules we would never think of making

A couples or family meeting, in itself, can create client assumptions of which a counsellor must be aware in order to prevent the counselling from doing harm. Clients may think they are receiving instructions or permission, even from a non-directive counsellor who intends neither. Without counsellor action or clarification they could assume any of the following:

- that the meeting is taking place because one of them is wrong, defective or the cause of the family's troubles (the counsellor may actively inquire about the wants and worries of every family member present rather than facilitate a meeting about the problems of just one person);
- that they would expose *every* worry or feeling about themselves or their significant others, feeling that they have no responsibility for discrimination in their conversation (the counsellor may take an active role which facilitates dialogue rather than monologue. Questions that ask for specifics or invite responses from others may reduce the threatening, evaluative conversations that can drive people apart);
- that the relational counsellor, despite claims to the contrary, is judging them as inadequate or will take responsibility to judge whether they or their adversary is correct (by responding with brief but clear explanations of her role or by matter-of-fact descriptions of the process, the counsellor may reduce anxiety or fear of judgement);
- that fellow family members or a partner will automatically be able to hear the hurt under their angry accusations and the longing for acceptance that is the source of their aggressively rejecting language. (By empathic responses to the feeling side of what is

> expressed and by acknowledging the reasonableness of the different points of view, the counsellor may facilitate the transformation of attacks into communication.)

Teach or model the basic skills of our work

It is the goal of the counselling that the family will self-regulate, make space for one another, and speak in statements that reveal individual predicaments rather than statements that shame and accuse others. In early sessions especially, the facilitator is active in reflecting a sense that something is *true for the speaker*, but is not necessarily *the truth*. Bernard Guerney, who integrated client-centred principles into a skills-building process called 'Relationship Enhancement Therapy', has emphasized the importance of teaching clients the difference between *subjective* statements, which claim only to represent the speaker's own point of view, and objective statements, which attempt to define only one possible truth (Guerney, 1998). Permission to hear another without threat to your own integrity or freedom creates safety for dialogue. In the following statements the counsellor is modelling respect for each person along with awareness of the possibility of a totally different perspective:

- Let's hear out Lucy completely, Harold, then you will have a chance to express your point of view.
- When that happened, independent of Mary's intention, you felt: 'Well, she must have no respect for me at all'.
- From your point of view, right now, there doesn't seem to be much chance for the marriage to continue. The experience that most leads you to say that is . . . ?
- Rob and I are going to listen, while you talk about what is going on from the parent's point of view. Later you and I will listen to see if there is a difference from the teenager's point of view.
- Margaret, I am not here as a judge. I am going to listen to Fred about what is important to him for me to know about how your behaviour seemed to him. I am also going to listen to you about whatever you want me to know about what's important to you. Can we work it that way?

Explain, but do not overexplain

The counsellor makes sense out of the session by responding to what each person has said is his/her reason for being there. For those

unable to verbalize their own reasons for coming, he offers appreciation for their being present because others have asked them to be.
The following are some statements intended to include and reassure
more reluctant members:

- I'm glad you are here. I appreciate that this may not be how you
  would have chosen to spend the afternoon. It's important to your
  mother that you are here to be in on this conversation about how
  your family works. From time to time I may ask you if you want
  to comment or ask a question, in case you find there is something
  you want to say.
- I have found that even though conversation in these meetings can
  be awkward and uncomfortable, sometimes families are glad that
  they have them because they find out more about what everybody else in the family has been thinking about.
- Everybody here may have a different thought about what the
  problem is in the family. Sometimes it might seem that people are
  pointing fingers at the person they believe is to blame – and it
  may look like they are saying the problem is all because of you. If
  anyone feels that is happening let me know and we will make
  sure that you have a chance to say what it's like from your point
  of view.

The counsellor's explanations can reduce anxiety – and especially in
the first two sessions explicitly reassure people that he is not a judge
taking people's sides. This may be less necessary in later sessions, but
the function of explaining continues to be a resource that the counsellor can offer that makes it possible for clients to handle emotionally charged issues without a sense of being assaulted. She may
say in a later session:

> I think we are on a subject about which there are a lot of strong feelings.
> I'm feeling we are being pretty brave to be talking about this and I
> appreciate everyone staying in the room while facing this hard subject.

In another context, talking about first sessions in individual
counselling, Mearns and Thorne have remarked: 'No matter what
happens both parties can maintain "face" and this can often be of
particular importance for the client in the beginning stages of a
counselling relationship' (Mearns and Thorne, 1988: 108). The counsellor does not have control over every person maintaining face in
the sometimes rough give-and-take of a counselling relationship.
And she cannot know what can be tolerated in some families who
have, what seems to her to be, a rude style of confronting each other.

She is not there to teach good manners but she can check with clients about their tolerance and encourage them to make choices about what they can handle at any one time. I might give a seemingly alienated client a choice over how we may talk about an issue:

> We can stay with this topic, Dave, about which Marie has a lot to say, or if you like, I can ask some questions to go at it in a slightly different way.

The counsellor must beware of the danger that her own anxiety level will lead her to talk so much that the clients are distracted from their own experiencing and intentions. Disturbing differences between clients that are the reason for the counselling must be understood to each person's satisfaction before a middle ground can be discovered. The counsellor, of course, will have to get feedback about her use of either too much explanation or too little. The counsellor who explains too much will convey mistrust in the clients' own ability to make sense out of the counselling. The counsellor who explains too little may discourage clients by failing to contribute her own answers to 'Why are we here? What can we accomplish?'

Bring up or encourage intellectual constructs to make sense out of the material of the session

As counselling progresses, couples and family members become able to bring their own images or ideas to make sense out of the disorder in which they may be caught. However, in the first sessions the counsellor may offer perspectives that are not presented as the truth, but as a way of looking at the situation that relieves anxiety and increases a sense of possibility in the meeting. In this example the counsellor anticipates some of the complexity and anxiety of the session:

> There are three things many families usually try to do in beginning counselling. One is to talk about difficult and frustrating problems without having to pretend things are better than they are. The second is to figure out how to give everyone a chance to say what it's like from their own chair. The third is to not leave here feeling like you are going nuts. At the end of the session, I'd like to check in on how we did on all three. (Oh you came in here already nuts? Then we won't have to worry about that one!)

In the next statement, the counsellor gives a matter-of-fact description of a stuck point in a conversation and implies that counselling is about finding a new way:

This seems like what often happens when people get onto the topic of drinking. Both of you look very discouraged and it seems to me that we are getting into the kind of conversation you have had dozens of times before. ('Dozens? How about hundreds?' might be a typical response from a member of a couple momentarily lost in his usual dreary role.)

Variations on the following lengthy speech have been very soothing to couples who get quickly discouraged if, in the first session, they see no alternative to trying to force a quick agreement about a complex problem (see Farson, 1996: 42 and Chapter 8 in this book for further discussion of this concept):

> My friend Dick Farson likes to quote the philosopher Abraham Kaplan's idea that people have both *problems* and *predicaments*. A *problem* is something outside yourself that you can figure out and just do something about. A *predicament* is something that involves you and something or someone you love, like how to be in a marriage or how to be a parent. You can't just solve a predicament; you have to figure out how to cope with it. We are here trying to sort out what are problems that each of you can solve by doing this or that; and what are predicaments that we have to understand by listening to each other and listening to ourselves without having any immediate solution.

Be sensitive to the family member's fear of being judged

As in all good person-centred counselling, the counsellor's personal feelings and reactions create a genuine relationship with clients. Her humour, openness and welcoming words reassure clients that they are not in the hands of a distant superior bureaucrat. She also uses her feelings to sense safety issues, dangers to self-esteem, double messages and discouraging words. In the first example, the counsellor feels different and conflicting needs from his clients:

> I feel a lot of urgency from you, Cathy, to be heard all the way through; and you, Ted, look kind of uncomfortable and under attack. Have I got that right? Could you, Ted, tolerate Cathy's telling me the one most urgent thing she wants you to know, if we then take time to focus on what that means to you? Would that be possible for you, for now, Cathy?

In the second example, the counsellor tunes in to the atmosphere he feels is shared by both:

> As I listen here, I get a sinking feeling. This conversation feels sad to me. It seems as though you both have been very discouraged, each in your own private way, ever since you had that conversation.

In this next example, Norm Chambers (1998) highlights a predicament that may be experienced by every relational counsellor:

> I am seeing a great-grandmother and her two great-grandchildren – the third generation of children she is raising. Wonderful loving woman. As she talks however, she keeps saying that one of the boys, Brian, is the smart one, and has a much easier, more successful time than Ken his brother. Each time she speaks like this, I can see Ken shrinking in his chair and I cringe, but I don't want to shame this good-intentioned woman.
>
> Later on in the session, I get with her alone and ask if there are some good qualities that Ken has. 'Oh yes,' she tells me. 'He is wonderful at fixing things; and he is so funny; and he is the one who asks if he can help me.' I asked her if she could mention some of those things when she mentions how smart Brian is and she said 'Oh yes!'

Every relational counsellor will occasionally have to deal with strong discomfort about one client's language becoming insulting, demeaning, or apparently unfair to another client, whether or not he intends it. Norm was able to deal with his discomfort without any blame. In early-stage relational counselling, 'I' statements about what you are experiencing may signify judgement to one or more clients. Norm might have shamed the grandmother if he had said: 'I feel uncomfortable about your comparing the intelligence of Ken and Brian'. For another example, to say 'I feel uncomfortable when you raise your voice like that,' may be helpful in a situation in which the counsellor's unconditional positive regard and refusal to judge has already been established. In early sessions, however, such 'I' statements may cast the counsellor into the role of either a victim or a scold and increase the defensiveness of the speaker. For example:

> *Counsellor*: I feel uncomfortable when you label Billy in such definite terms.
> *Billy's mother*: Well, good for you! What the hell are we supposed to do here anyway?

Instead, the counsellor may refer in a matter-of-fact way to the requirements of the situation:

> In these first sessions, we have the job of getting everybody's story out without driving anyone out of the room. Can you tell the story directly to me, George, so that Sally doesn't have to take it in as though she is on trial?

Or:

> In this first session, I want to have the chance to hear what bothers everyone. I also want to ask about other sides of this, like what in this marriage made you want to come in and look for counselling?

Or simply:

> How are we doing at talking about this touchy area? I'm concerned that you, Bob, look kind of shut down. Are you here with us or have you gone away?

Anticipate client concerns about inclusion and fairness

When I have seen clients for individual counselling more than two or three times and they ask to move into couples work, I generally suggest that they go to another counsellor for that purpose. Sometimes, the other partner will still want to try the counselling with me and I am willing to agree as long as we are open to evaluating it as it unfolds. In some cases, I will find that in talking to one person I feel so aligned with her individual interests that I would be unable to be a fair witness for the two of them. In any event, I usually offer the new partner a session alone with me so that he can find his own connection and make his own assessment. The freedom to choose is more important than whether or not he uses the chance. Here is an example of the idiosyncratic process of forming a therapeutic alliance with more than one person:

> I saw a couple, one of whom was a woman I had seen two years before for individual counselling. When she appeared with her new husband I extended him the invitation to talk individually so that he could feel I had made a connection with him to begin to balance my connection with his partner. His attention was entirely on the conversation he wanted to have with his wife and he politely shrugged off the chance to talk alone with me. For him, trust-building with me was irrelevant. He was able to take his wife's word for my trustworthiness, was satisfied by a brief exchange with me, or was so ready to engage with his wife that any attempted first session ritual would have been like giving a carrot to a galloping horse. At a later time, however, he asked for an individual session for an issue he felt belonged more to him than to the couple. He wanted equal time only for his own support and learning, not out of concern about whose side I was on.

With some couples, trust is so volatile an issue that seeing either alone, even once, interferes with the counselling. It is not uncommon, after a first session, to get a call from one of the partners asking for an individual session. I am usually positive and confirming about their desire to work on many issues in many different ways. I also usually ask that we postpone such meetings while the counselling with the couple is our focus. Later, when trust is well established and clients have defined individual areas to work on, I may agree to individual work.

Be hopeful

Hopefulness is at the heart of counselling. It is the unexpressed other side of all the bad news our clients initially share in our offices. It is as if they were saying: 'All these terrible things are true between us and yet here we all are in your office tentatively expecting that something different may happen.' Carl Rogers expresses this hopefulness from his work with individuals and in groups:

> I have often pointed out that in my work with individuals in therapy and in my experience in encounter groups, I have been led to the conviction that human nature is essentially constructive. When, in a therapeutic climate (which can be objectively defined) a person becomes sharply aware of more of his or her internal experiencing and of the stimuli and demands from the external world, thus acquiring a full range of options, the person tends to move in the direction of becoming a socially constructive organism. (Rogers, 1978: 23)

When clients first come in, it is sometimes difficult for beginning relational counsellors not to be discouraged by client anger, rigidity, fear and judgement. In early sessions the counsellor learns to be confident in an alternate story which will emerge as clients become trusting in the counselling process. The following ideas, supported by experience, keep me grounded, patient and expectant of the clients' ability to make use of relational counselling.

1. Clients have an unspoken other side which brought them there to begin with. As couples therapist Richard Stuart has said, the person most reluctant for more togetherness has some wish for connection and interdependence; the person most eager for connection and interdependence has some wish for separateness and individuality (Stuart, 1989).
2. Most clients expect the counsellor to be able to somehow be fair and helpful to their apparent adversary even while initially *seeming* to demand that the counsellor take their side and their side alone.
3. Clients can be moved by unexpected chances to glimpse the undefensive emotional statement of their partner. One client told his wife and me, 'When I heard how her heart was breaking, I could no longer manage to be cynical.'

4. Clients are often softer and more able to admit their contribution to the trouble after they are allowed the chance to express their judgemental one-sided view of things.
5. Many clients have in the past surprised themselves and their significant others by congruent, non-judgemental, creative, disarming words and actions. They have managed to win each other over; remain lovers during transition periods; get older together; raise and like children during at least part of their lives; pay rents or mortgages; live in the same house; and adjust to the tolerance of the hundreds of habits which make up a human life. They are there in your presence because they are blocked from the resources they have which would allow them to continue.

Close the session so that its relationship to the clients' purpose in being there is acknowledged

It is *very* important to leave plenty of time for closing a first session with a couple or family. It is easy to underestimate the value of good timekeeping. Without it, vital issues like the time of the next appointment, who should be included, and important client feedback will be pre-empted by the arrival of the next clients. The counsellor may want to check with each person if there is anything they want to say. Sometimes a misunderstanding may be uncovered that would otherwise have caused one family member to leave angry or hurt (the counsellor cannot prevent family members from leaving angry and hurt, but would prefer it not be because they wrongly thought he had targeted one of them as to blame for the whole problem!). There may be an important topic that, if not discussed, would lead one or more members to feel the counsellor had failed to grasp their purpose in being there.

The counsellor may share topics that she noticed were mentioned but were not followed up. She may ask if people are comfortable enough to meet again and answer questions or facilitate discussion about how long the counselling is likely to continue.

Norm Chambers often tells a couple that he works best if they can commit to six sessions of work with him. 'After the six sessions we can determine whether or not to go forward.' A commitment for more than one session can create safety for a couple to feel more free to explore difficult topics which they might avoid if they were fearful that their partner was deciding from moment to moment whether or not to stay. 'What do you do if they only want to commit to one more session?' Norm was asked. He replied, 'I agree to meet with them, but it changes how I might be with them.' If a couple are likely to come for only one more session, Norm is likely to structure more, say more and facilitate more closure. With a commitment of six sessions there is much more room and safety for complex, difficult-to-resolve issues to emerge and be processed with less counsellor activity.

Counsellors may consider offering a summary of the session and what it has accomplished in relation to clients' stated goals. Person-centred relational counselling holds the tension between boundary-less existential exploration and a somewhat safe attempt to increase meaningful exchanges between people who live together. Often there is both surprising exploration and concern for safety, independent of the counsellor's intention, but in the first session I lean toward the latter. 'How do you end sessions?' I asked Breffni Barrett, who replied:

> I tell a story about the family. I reframe the problem so there is some hopefulness. I ask if they are comfortable with coming. I let them know that I have some ideas about how we can fix things. I leave them with something tangible. I don't leave them wondering 'What the hell happened?'

How do *I* end first sessions? I try to give families and couples an idea of what to expect. For example, to a mother and two boys, aged 16 and 12:

> This is what it would be like if we continue. It's different from individual counselling and it's different from taking one of you to a doctor to be fixed. We would be likely to keep talking about what happens for each of you when things get bad and what happens – what each of you do – when things get better. It's different from just talking about one person's problems. I will be in here, giving my opinions with the rest of you; I'll also be asking you what your opinions are. I am particularly interested, with three people like you, in helping you understand what it's like for the other family members.

I attempt to get impressions of what the experience has been like. I would rather a family discuss what was left out or what was offensive there in my presence than in the car as they drive away. In this way, I also model a process for family and couple discussions outside of counselling. Can they learn to complete a conversation by acknowledging what they accomplished, what was missing and what was unfinished? In the middle stages of counselling, as described in Chapter 7, counselling becomes more reflective of the nature and style of each couple or family.

CHAPTER 7

In the Middle of Relational Counselling

Family and couples counselling tends to be of shorter duration than individual counselling. Significant learning may take place even in one to three meetings. In his course on Theories of Marriage and Family Therapy (United States International University, Fall 1981), James Framo painted a picture of a family driving home from a therapist and the father saying something like:

> Seventy-five bucks an hour! From now on I'm going to be spending more time at home, I want to talk more and listen more with you, Marie. And you kids . . . I'm going to expect you to do your part and I will listen to you more about what you need from me. What do you say?

In my practice, many couples and families will meet for six to 15 sessions. Often these meetings, after two or three weekly sessions, will take place every two weeks so that the counselling extends to four months or more. Some couples and a few families will meet over a time extending to a year or more. Frequently, family counselling will become couples counselling with occasional visits by the children. At times, couples counselling will become individual counselling. In all these meetings there is a describable middle of counselling. This chapter describes characteristics I have found repeatedly in the middle stage of counselling.

More complexity develops around issues

Unreflective, mutually blaming, unequivocal characterizations, draconian attempts to control one another, and acting out rather than sharing of feelings often give way in the middle of counselling to a different type of dialogue. In early sessions a person might be inclined to say: 'If you don't stop drinking, I am going to leave you.' In middle sessions, the same partner might say:

> I'm not going to leave you over your drinking right now. I really, really hate how you are when you drink, but I enjoy you a lot when you are not drinking. Besides, I'm not into moving into a small flat with two kids right now. But I'm not making any promises either. I'm not going to live the way I've been living, that's the one thing I'm sure of. I don't know how it's going to work out in the long run.

This client has shifted herself from a position to a person. She is neither placating nor attempting to control through threat. She is making her own evaluations rather than accepting her partner's or those of the chorus of advisors who frequently surround a relationship. She has opened a new position in the system in which she decides herself what is in her best interest rather than following anyone else's formula. Her partner is off the hook in terms of her immediate attempt to control him; but he is faced with the unsettling reality that he does not know what she will do next. He may be disarmed and freer to enjoy and respect his partner. He also has to contend with a real person rather than someone who predictably cooperates with his own ebb and flow of placation and defiance.

One older couple, who had met frequently over years with their adult son and his counsellor, had always made choices about what financial support to give to their son based on the state of their approval of his behaviour and intentions. In one important session, well into the counselling relationship, after trust had been established, one of his requests for money touched a chord regarding their own situation rather than their duties as parents. 'How much money do you think we have?' the father was able to ask. 'We could never afford to give you that!' the mother was able to say. Their son was strengthened and empowered and sympathetic as, putting aside the question of what was good or bad for him, they became persons with needs rather than an inexhaustible resource. In the middle of counselling, *trouble* can become useable for growth because it can be congruently expressed rather than concealed in controlling language.

The counsellor himself is often surprised by dimensions that are revealed as counselling continues. He may be convinced that one member of a couple is the one who was most dismayed by the unexpected arrival of a child and find that the other had, early in life, vowed 'never to have children'. He may find that the quiet gentle member of a couple struggles the most with periods of rage. The counsellor has facilitated the experience of safety that allows greater self-disclosure.

Strong feelings emerge – sometimes unexpectedly

As clients are more comfortable they sometimes get in touch with deeply felt disappointments. In a safe atmosphere a client may surprise his significant others, the counsellor and sometimes himself by the depth of frustration and rage which can emerge. This rage should neither be seen as regression nor taken literally to be about something wrong with a family member. In middle sessions, the counsellor may see anger as an expression of freedom to raise deeper concerns. If facilitated rather than just vented on a reactive significant other, rage can be a gateway to discussion of significant hurt, unfinished business or grief. For example:

> *A client may say about her husband*: I'll tell you right away. I feel like this has been a waste of time. I don't like him and I don't want to bother anymore with a relationship that has been a mismatch since the beginning.
>
> *The counsellor may reply*: Something we are talking about right now seems to have *really* bothered you. You are discouraged and wanting to pull away because of something you are experiencing.

Or the following:

> *A client may say*: I'll tell you this! You are a controlling bitch. You've been that all your life. You aren't going to change.
>
> *To which the counsellor may say*: That came out strong and extremely frustrated and you have all our attention. What do you want us to know? (*The 'us' is a reminder that the anger is an event in counselling, not a one-sided attack on a partner.*)

The counsellor may respond differently in middle sessions than in a first session. She has developed a relationship with both speaking and listening clients. Unconditional acceptance of emerging feelings *does not exclude* accountability for honest subjective expression rather than insulting, ranting and raving. In their listening, clients may have learned to be less immediately reactive to what their significant others share and that the counsellor can be trustworthy during risky exploration. More concretely, each has learned that *everyone* gets a hearing every session if she wants it. Rage is usually harmful in monologue and often helpful in dialogue. If it emerges when trust is high and clients are self-directing, all that is needed is: 'What's up?'; or ' I think you have the floor'; or 'I'm interested in what's happening with you right now. You seem deeply hopeless about something.' It is often useful for the counsellor to place the expression of anger in a context as he does in the following example:

> Let me go back over where this conversation has been. Rick said he wanted to talk about his need to concentrate on work this month especially. Betty said that she wanted more time with just Rick and her. Rick thought that would be a good idea and 'could they plan it for after the twenty-fifth?' Betty said that will be fine. Rick said he wishes Betty could be more supportive about his work. *Betty said that she doesn't know why she even bothers to be in the relationship*. Shall we go back to you, Betty, about what you heard when Rick brought up the word supportive at

work? Or should we go to you, Rick, about what you meant when you brought it up?'

As in individual work, relational counselling, in middle sessions, becomes a place in which one learns by attending without judgement to the surprising feelings that emerge in conversation. Different from individual counselling is the counsellor's need to turn from the expressing person to his listeners so that strong personal feelings become intelligible in the relationship.

Clients have a crisis and get through it

In the middle of relational counselling, clients will frequently have a crisis in which the situation between or among them seems to get worse rather than better. In fact, clients may feel that moments of peace and harmony before the crisis were ironic or, worse, hypocritical as divisions are exaggerated and behaviour is distancing, demeaning or untrustworthy. For example:

- a partner will reveal that he has chosen to leave the relationship and that he is still connected with another person with whom he has denied a relationship;
- a teenager will get into a fight with a teacher and be suspended or expelled from school;
- someone will get drunk and, repeating an old pattern, not come home one night;
- a teenager will threaten suicide to his friends and then disappear;
- one partner will shout that divorce is the only answer; or
- less dramatically and most commonly, one person may complain bitterly that he or she feels like the only one making any effort at change.

Sometimes, the counsellor makes little or no direct contribution to the resolution of the crisis, other than to be there for each member of the group. The counselling itself, however, may lead to change that not only resolves the crisis but reduces the family or couple's discouragement:

- one or more clients will attempt to understand rather than just attack or defend;
- one or more clients will make an unexpected effort or play an unanticipated role;

- one or more clients will make a statement of unconditional love; or
- one or more clients will be assertive and refrain from rescuing or placating in their usual ways.

For example, one member of a couple got into a car in the middle of the night. The other figured out where she was going and found her – they had an all-night conversation in a supermarket parking lot. A father tracked down his suicidal son and talked with him, acknowledging some of his grievances and asking for and giving a commitment to work things out. I know another father who once walked silently with his son around dark city streets through much of a night after the son had been arrested for minor theft. He didn't say much; the first thing he said was, 'I'm going to stay with you tonight until you are ready to go home'. Crises can remind people that they love each other underneath it all.

At other times, the counsellor is central in the resolution of a crisis. He may, as in Box 7.1, facilitate a conversation in which clients feel able to be vulnerable enough to share important connecting feelings.

Box 7.1 Would I feel differently if I knew you loved me?

In the eighth month of counselling, a couple came in to each announce that there was no sense in continuing the relationship. They each shared a skilled caricature of the other. Ellen felt that she had done all the giving, all the listening, all the trying. In Ellen's eyes, Ralph was married to routine. Emotionally cut off from others, he would emerge periodically for sex or for someone to listen to his interminable stories. He was unable to see her as another person; he had no appreciation of her; she was just a worker who followed his orders. She could stay married to him only if she gave up the idea that there was such a thing as intimacy; or that there was any hope at all that she could be loved by someone who could really see her.

Ralph was not at a loss for words about Ellen. He saw her as more selfish than he ever had imagined she could be. She was a self-absorbed prima donna who expected him to stand on his head for her; earn all the money; do all the household work; take care of the children; and learn to talk in the same language as her friends with whom she sat drinking cappuccinos while he was out earning a living.

Ellen agreed with only these words of Ralph's: 'I can't go on forever like this. After a while, you just don't want to bother. It's all one-sided and I would be a fool to hang around much longer.'

There was one other thing that the couple agreed on. They were both certain that the other one no longer loved them and was no longer interested in them.

The counsellor heard a version of this statement from each and asked them both a question: 'If you felt that you were wrong about this, and Ellen (Ralph) really did turn out to love you, would that make it worthwhile to continue?' Only after much assurance that it was understood that clearly the other did not, could not, love them, did each say that the other loving them would make a difference to how they felt. Each dared further to say explicitly that they would want to stay in the relationship if the other one wanted to. There, in the midst of the crisis emerged the admission that each *would* want the other if the other *could* love them. This and other *softening* statements (Johnson and Greenberg, 1994a) allowed connection to continue during the confusion and storm of the middle of counselling.

For some couples, however, a crisis will lead to the realization for one or more parties that a relationship cannot be continued. For example, a client who was defensive for a while about her inability to keep her side of agreements made in the counselling, may share the realization that she is no longer really willing to invest in the relationship with her current partner. Another client, after trying on various ways of looking at what love might mean, says: 'I'm sorry. I've tried. I probably haven't tried hard enough, but I don't think it should be this hard. My heart just isn't in it.' Frequently that statement will represent a permanent resolution of her ambivalence about the relationship. Less often, having had permission to voice such a clear choice, a client may allow suppressed feelings in favour of the relationship to emerge and decide the issue. Sometimes it is only when clients actually voice a decision that they know whether it is right or wrong.

Some clients will find, in the middle of counselling, a sense of such fundamental differences that they feel closure on the effort to stay together. In a good experience of counselling, clients can learn that even under supportive conditions they cannot find joy or purpose in the relationship. It is never for the counsellor to draw this conclusion or attempt to bring it about; and it is not for the counsellor to work to prevent it other than by the honest facilitation and feedback that asks clients to look at the bases for their decisions.

Some clients are threatened and withdraw in the middle of counselling

As some clients become more comfortable and proactive in the middle of relational counselling, others may feel so anxious that they stop the counselling either by not showing up for their next appointment or cancelling without re-scheduling. A session that for the professional may seem straightforward and helpful may bring a couple or family to the brink of issues that one or more of them do not want to face. The counselling may reveal fault lines in a relationship which later will lead one partner either to make a major life change or to decide to stay in a relationship with the confirmed belief that some issues cannot ever be dealt with thoroughly or even openly.

Some clients see a process orientation, in itself, as a threat to their personal power, to their sense of worth, and in particular to their place in the family relationship. Less outwardly rigid members of families may react more subtly and politely, but still feel that listening without judgement to everyone's feelings may mean the end of what they consider to be a stable and good family life. For example, in the mid-life counselling of a couple who had lived in a hierarchy which placed the husband as the authority on financial matters, issues of equal decision-making, intellectually convincing as they might be, represented a threat to that husband's sense of well-being (see Box 7.2).

Box 7.2   This is as far as we will go

Joyce: I'm a grown-up now. Life is short. When you come home with a new computer without asking me, I wonder, 'What am I doing here? Am I one of the kids?'

Phil: I can see how you might feel that way. I thought we had talked about it. The kids had been on my back. I asked you to come with me when I read there was a sale at Computerland.

Joyce: If you did, it was just before Passover and I was busy – Passover was at our house this year, remember? I didn't have time. Besides, I had already told you that I didn't want to spend the money. Suddenly, there you were installing a new Hewlett-Packard with money I wanted to use for carpeting. And you moved out the little Macintosh that I had just gotten used to. And did you ask me last year to come with you when you bought the Taurus? Or when you bought the washing machine?

Phil: [*looks uncomfortable*]

Counsellor [*aware both of Joyce's eagerness to bring up the many ways over the years she has been ignored as a decision-maker and of Phil's discomfort in listening to an overwhelming list of accusations*]: Joyce, you feel very clear that Phil hasn't consulted you about important financial decisions.

Joyce: I'm sorry honey. I don't want to just attack you, but I had said, 'If you have to get a computer, get something second-hand.' So in you walk with this huge state-of-the-art monster.

Phil: It was the second cheapest one there. Jennifer was with me and she was pressuring me to get this new *NEC* and I was fighting her off and trying to keep in mind your feelings as well. It was the least elaborate thing I could find that Jennifer said would even help her a little.

Joyce: And then there's the washing machine. I'm the one that uses it.

Counsellor: Phil, what are you hearing from Joyce?

Phil: You think I feel I can make financial decisions by myself and that I do it without including you. I guess you are right.

Counsellor: You, Joyce, would like a change. You would like Phil and you to decide together what to buy.

Joyce: Well, it would be a nice change.

Counsellor [*reflecting nothing but body language*]: You, Phil, don't have any way to disagree with Joyce about this, but you are worried that this will bring a lot of discussion into the house that you are afraid you won't like.

Phil [*laughs and says eagerly*]: Yes! I'm not comfortable arguing. It seems like it's been easier and less complicated to just do things by myself.

The couple in this discussion did not return after that session, despite at closing and on follow-up many expressions of interest in continuing. The counsellor can control neither the extent to which one member of a family will bring up threatening material nor the extent to which another will tolerate it. The relational counsellor must live with uncertainty about whether issues initiated in counselling will be resolved, transformed, catalytic for one person's change or avoided at a higher cost because of the counselling.

The core conditions are expressed differently in the middle of relational counselling

The middle of relational counselling may be characterized by the following:

- increased trust of the counsellor and the counselling process by all participants;
- the counsellor more frequently in the background as family members are more able to talk directly with one another without the provocation that accompanies feelings of insecurity and fear of not being heard; and
- more ownership of the agenda by the clients.

The middle of counselling is like the working phase of a group in which issues of trust and competition have receded in favour of more direct sharing on issues. The counsellor, therefore, is less fixed in role and less held responsible for keeping the counselling 'on track'. In early sessions, some clients are preoccupied with whether or not a counselling session keeps focus on a narrowly defined topic. This concern can fade as trust builds and they see the counselling as an opportunity to share and learn without judgement.

The core conditions of the person-centred approach work dynamically as counselling progresses. For example, the more the counsellor is able to be self-aware and congruent with a family or couple, the less her self-consciousness will interfere. Less burdened by the need to prove her competence, she will understand her clients more accurately; and her responses will reach clients at a level deeper and more specific to them. The more she understands their point of view, the more natural her acceptance and warm positive regard will become. The following are reflections on the core conditions as they are manifested in middle sessions.

Empathy in middle sessions

The counsellor's empathic responses may become more intuitive and responsive to the uniqueness of each client present. She may be able to make more contact with each individual without other family members feeling she is neglecting them or taking someone's side. Whereas in early counselling she focuses on careful attention to the clients' words or spoken intentions, in the middle of counselling she may be able to respond additionally to the clients' deeper, more complex meanings just on the edge of their own awareness. She is free to do this because the clients trust her and are enough in the centre of their own *locus of evaluation* (Rogers, 1959) to take or leave what the counsellor offers. Empathy becomes a matter of seeing as well as hearing; putting things in context as well as appreciating the meaning of words and tone of voice.

In the middle sessions a counsellor may say:

- I am also picking up something else. Are you saying you would be much more expressive of your emotions if you weren't afraid that Sam would get uncomfortable and shut down?
- Wait a minute, what just happened? You said 'If I had *any voice* in this'. Did you hear that – *any voice*? Can you tell me more about *any voice*?
- Here is what I'm getting. Bill, 18, says (when his mother is driving his brother and him around a mountain town), 'We're going the wrong fucking direction'. Suddenly you are all idiots and you've just made the biggest mistake in the world. It seems like your job is to just feel bad and then try like anything to get on the right road. You're not allowed to stop the car and ask, 'What's going on here? Why are you talking to me like that?'

- I know this isn't our subject, but I keep sensing from you something like: 'I'm tired. I'm too tired to be any good in handling this predicament.' Does that make any sense to you?

The counsellor is freer to be more personal because the clients are more established in the counselling. There is more room for tracking individual persons as their significant others' initial anxiety makes room for more tolerance of new information. They come to expect appreciation and understanding of each client's unique reactions and accept this process as the road to relief from their frustration and alienation.

Congruence in the middle of counselling

Congruence, at this point, means that more of the unique qualities of the counsellor become part of the clients' experience. Counsellors for whom a sense of humour comes naturally may phrase things in eccentric or humorous ways and still remain true to their task of showing understanding of the uniqueness of the family. An ability to genuinely enjoy peculiarities can be confirming and reassuring to a family trapped in self-doubt and pessimism. Counsellors with a natural affinity for children can express that inclination and in the process form a bond with a whole family that draws out family energy and self-esteem. Counsellors who are emotionally expressive can respond to good or bad news with tears in a way that in an early session would be confusing or otherwise intrusive for clients.

The counsellor can share more reactions without seeming to impose diagnoses. When I first see a couple who are stuck on topics such as alcohol abuse or a suspected extra-relationship affair, I neither avoid the topic nor focus on it. In the mid-life of a counselling relationship, however, such perfected neutrality about opinion can become artificial. I am a person who cares and who has wishes that will emerge unless I aspire to be good at concealing or portraying something other than what I think and feel. Eventually, for example, certain clients are going to know that I wish they would stop drinking. A counsellor can be observant and frank while still refusing to reduce a person to any category or formulaic treatment plan. If it emerges that I am acting toward a person 'as if' he is alcoholic, then that is information that may be shared if it can be done without my joining forces with other family members against him. For example:

Do I also think you should be assessed by an alcohol treatment programme? Yeah. I wish you would. I also see that you really seem to hate the idea. Is that true? That you feel you would lose something very important if you were evaluated for alcoholism?

The counsellor is describing his reaction, not prescribing the client's plan of action. The urge to make one person do or be something different is already an inextricable part of family predicaments. What is helpful – what may be the art of a counselling that truly facilitates – is a process that includes counsellor openness and careful non-defensive attention to the meaning of his words to the client. It can be openly discussed: that the obese person avoids exercise; the alcoholic goes to a pub rather than goes home; the chronically unemployed person does not look for work; the authoritarian father yells at his second child even while feeling guilty over the same behaviour with his first. The persons who live with all of these people are discouraged by their way of acting, however detached from it they seek to be. The counsellor models a way of speaking for oneself without attempting to control another. That persons are not *only* obese, not *only* alcoholic, not *only* unemployed, not *only* authoritarian or not *only* victim of another family member's behaviour is also manifested in the counsellor's congruent interaction.

Unconditional positive regard is different in the middle of relational counselling

The longer the counselling lasts, the more tested the counsellor's unconditional positive regard will be as clients reveal their limits, their frustrations with one another, the problems they cannot solve and the decisions they cannot make. In the middle of counselling, the counsellor must also accept himself and the limits of his own power, as client progress becomes uncertain. I have often found that judgement of my clients had its source in judgement of my own adequacy as a counsellor. In the beginning of counselling, it is easy to accept people just as they are – if they were not incongruent why would they be there? At the end of counselling, closure is achieved by accepting the gains, gifts and disappointments of the process as equally prized steps toward learning and relationship. The middle of counselling is when I may subtly or not so subtly have conditions on my acceptance. Clients change; they take important steps; they seem to have great insight; they report increased closeness and meaning; and then in the next session they express despair or say they want to abandon their attempts at change! The counsellor who becomes addicted to positive outcomes can quickly find himself a disappointed parent who has choice only about whether he shows disapproval openly or covertly.

In *unspoken* conversation the counsellor may communicate, 'Didn't you just get past this last session? Didn't you agree that your wife could want something without you having to feel responsible for providing it? Don't you get it?' even while trying to portray understanding and patience. Without speaking, the client may think in return: 'What's the use of trying? Now I've got the counsellor on my back along with my wife. This is a waste of time', while listlessly agreeing that he might have missed something last session and asking the counsellor to go over it again. The counsellor's unconditional positive regard can be diminished by attachment to apparent client progress. He can be distracted from his role as a facilitator of the client's own ability to find a way to be in his significant relationship.

In middle sessions, the counsellor relates to clients' problems while conveying acceptance of them as persons distinct from their problems and their success in dealing with them. The counsellor may make this concrete by checking in with each person each session about their own state of being. Over even a few sessions, clients can experience being received and valued as themselves and are less threatened as their predicaments surface and are examined.

Clients can suffer with the paradox of feeling they *should* be able to solve a problem even as they feel absolutely *powerless* to do anything about it. Dick Farson (1987) has expressed this formulation as a condition of potential abuse: the sense one should control something – make a child stop crying or yelling – and the stronger sense that one *cannot* control something (except by force). The feeling that they *should* be able to do something – about an intimate's having an affair, drinking too much, being depressed, failing at school, not doing his share of work – but are unable to, alienates clients from their own voices and their own ability to see alternatives and their own power. The resentment at their powerlessness may also alienate them further from their loved one. This split between their self-concept and their ideal self is at the heart of the struggle in the middle of counselling. The counsellor can be very helpful with a matter-of-fact non-judgemental statement of their dilemma. For example:

> Right now you strongly want Billy [16] to be back in school. You are also unwilling to try to make him go by means of force or threats.

In the counsellor's words the client is a person living with one of the complex realities of his life, rather than a fool or a failure or one of several other names an anxious person may call himself.

Frequent non-judgemental description of the progress of family communication by the counsellor can facilitate understanding and objectivity and gradually replace the need to judge in a couple or family. A simple history of where a conversation started and where it went can help clients get in touch with their original purpose rather than only their emotional reactions to the give-and-take of conversation. Awareness of the context allows clients to be freer from a sense of who is to blame or who is right or wrong:

> We started this conversation because both of you were frustrated with managing to take care of little Laura when she gets sick at daycare. You, Phil, said that you definitely couldn't be called at work without a lot of disruption taking place. You, Julia, took that to mean that Phil expected you to be 100 per cent on call if the daycare person needed to call one of you. I count three things on the table: responsibility for Laura during the day; Phil's work situation and pressure not to be interrupted; and Julia's desire for fairness in sharing responsibility for Laura, and her feeling that she is left with that responsibility by default.

By keeping track of the flow of conversation, the person-centred counsellor can model interest in a new experience between clients rather than the unprocessed automatic emotional reactions which make conversations disintegrate. In the middle of counselling the clients' experience of a non-judgemental, acceptant atmosphere allows for increasingly natural expression of genuine thoughts and feelings. Clients are able to be more than their roles – less bound by strategy and more open to the change in perspective which is the great accomplishment of relational counselling.

The definition of the presenting problem expands and is clarified

In the middle of counselling, the clients continually redefine the presenting problem as each voice is heard and the conversation becomes more congruent. *Again and again in relational counselling clients can be vulnerable to the feeling that they are not accomplishing anything if they are not able to assert control over their own or others' behaviour.* I believe it is very important for the counsellor to acknowledge progress in relation to the presenting problem. In middle sessions, clients are doing the real work of counselling by struggling to express or hear each person's side of a confusing issue, but can feel as though they are wasting time or are somehow failing. The counsellor's empathy may take the form of relating seemingly irrelevant communications to attempts to make a difference in the family's distress.

Relational counselling usually begins with a presenting problem that is articulated by one family member and more or less supported by other family members. In conversation, a general problem turns into several presenting problems: at least one for each member of the couple or family. The back and forth of the counselling conversation leads to more complex articulation and expansion of the differing views of the problem. By the middle of counselling clients have often increased ability to express their problem in subjective terms rather than as objective fact; and their significant others are more frequently able to listen to the other's point of view with less defensiveness. In the progress of counselling a problem may take five different forms:

1. a narrow, accusatory definition;
2. a broader, more subjective perspective in which more personal elements of the problem are expressed by each participant;
3. a deeper expression of individual core issues related to the problem which may have pre-existed the problem;
4. a recognition of the way in which each individual's manner of expression and interpretation co-create moments of frustration and conflict; and
5. a recognition of possible individual efforts which would change the nature of the presenting problem.

Box 7.3 gives an example of this process.

Box 7.3   Dialogue itself reframes a problem

The original presenting problem for Marie and Lisa is constant arguing. Under conditions favouring dialogue, the definition of the problem is expanded and clarified:

- Marie at first defines the cause of the arguing to be Lisa's lack of concern about her needs and wishes. Lisa sees the cause as Marie's never-ending, always changing demands.
- Further dialogue defines part of the problem as Marie's hurt at feeling overlooked; her fear that indeed she never will be satisfied; and her longing for company and closeness. Lisa's side of the problem is her fear of failure and of letting an important person down. She reveals that she hears any disappointment in Marie's life as a criticism.
- Marie later reveals that she fears Lisa has lost interest in her. Lisa admits that she doubts whether Marie respects anything that she has done, is doing, or will do.
- Marie tells of a lifelong fear of reliving the life of her apparently chronically complaining, lonely and fearful mother. Lisa shares her struggle not to be like her withdrawn, sour and television-addicted father.

- Marie notices that she and Lisa couldn't be as bad as the roles 'we've gotten into: she's not the passive, negative do-nothing I keep picturing her as; I'm not the demanding bitch that she seems to see me as.'
- Later discussion finds Marie saying she needs to pick better times to talk about her discontents; to remember to tell Lisa when she is feeling more satisfied and to remember to say 'I want' at least as often as she says 'we should'. Lisa defines her tasks as: to listen to Marie without feeling she has to agree with her or comply with her wishes; to notice when she feels defensive and to check on whether Marie intends to be attacking; and to listen to her partner's feelings without judging or feeling judged.

As members of a family feel listened to and understood, they can allow more personal, less accusatory issues to enter the conversation. As they feel less judged, they are more likely to take responsibility for part of the problem. They may also, however, feel provoked back to a narrow blaming perspective.

The counsellor comments frequently on shifts in the nature of the conversation, inviting client observation and exploration of their own process. If a client accuses, the counsellor may ask what thought or feeling the client is experiencing. The client may articulate the feeling of anger, sadness or hurt and move into a more personally expressive mode. The counsellor does not see the client as deficient for being accusatory; he does ask him to go further with it. It is very hard to talk about sensitive issues without at some time regressing to blame, discouraged withdrawal and/or a short memory for constructive efforts. The counsellor is also needed as a witness to the fact that clients are works in progress rather than failures doomed to the same static style. Her commentary makes the counselling an event rather than a dreary repetition. For example:

To a husband who brings up feelings about his own parents: Russ, are you adding another element here? Some of the shame you feel is not just because Kathy criticizes you, but because of your sense that your father always disapproved of you?

To a mother who becomes reflective about her son's closeness to adulthood: Are you saying that you would rather Phil would say he disagrees with you directly than get a 'yes' you don't believe? Are you saying that you would be able to accept that kind of change in your relationship? [This last question makes explicit the shift that her statement implies.]

To a whole family in which a mother has become very discouraged: Let me just say what I've been seeing while I still remember it. Is it true that Bob has been talking more and saying more about what he wants than in any of our previous sessions? Haven't we moved from where Bob wasn't saying anything to another level in which Bob is saying things that Sally doesn't agree with, but he is able to keep talking?

In the middle of counselling, clients engage with their problems by changing the nature of their conversation about those problems. The counsellor affirms this process by acknowledging differences in the content and effect of the communication and inviting client reflection on the here-and-now activity of themselves and their significant others. The middle of counselling at best leads clients to a sense of their efficacy in relation to their problems and predicaments. Chapter 8 discusses issues and behaviours associated with the end of relational counselling.

CHAPTER 8

Ending Relational Counselling

I end couples and family counselling with clients when they want to end. It is probably the most client-centred part of my counselling. David Sanders says that the goal of relational therapy is for families and couples to 'get back into their own course of development'. The family's choice of how to live belongs to them. They come for counselling when something goes wrong from their point of view. When that is resolved they move forward in their own way. The counsellor follows their lead, not her ideal of what a relationship can be. Indeed, says Sanders, 'One family or couple might *end* at a point which for another would be a good *starting point* for therapy.' The relational counsellor must 'pare down expectations'.

I have frequently found that couples or family counselling is organized around getting over one problem or coming to terms with one predicament. When that is resolved or lived through, clients may intend 'deeper work' but the motivation is lessened, and they will tend to drift away from the counselling. For example, a couple may come in filled with mutual rage and frustration at the time of a bankruptcy after a job loss and unexpected loss of value of their property. The rage will affect their sex life and their ability to listen to each other. It frequently might make a woman regress to the very patterns she most hated in her mother and a man find himself imitating the very worst habits of his father. The counselling will serve the purpose of soothing their anxiety; allowing a discussion that is not about who is right or wrong; and creating the possibility that their trouble belongs more to their immediate situation than to their long-term character. One client said, 'We aren't finished with counselling by any means, but we need a break from it now that we are handling things better.'

Clients need support at different times in their lives and, having received it, prefer to continue with their own way of solving their problems. To try to insist that a couple or family continue because they need to resolve underlying issues implies that the counsellor possesses the expertise to know better than the clients what help they need. In Box 8.1 is an example of counselling ending even while a new phase is beginning.

Box 8.1   An ending session in which a small family begins to widen the family conversation

A lesbian mother, Sally, and her 12-year-old daughter, Melissa, had been meeting for several sessions to discuss Melissa's behaviour at school. We also discussed her relationship with grandparents and relationship with her somewhat distant father. Most important to Melissa was her feeling that Sally didn't give her enough attention and wasn't emotionally there enough for her. Sally had been gradually becoming more and more involved with Claire, her first steady partner since coming out. Sally included Claire in many activities with Melissa; Melissa was ambivalent about this.

During the course of the counselling, Melissa was able to talk about the fact that her mother's differentness embarrassed her at times. They were in a city in which homosexuality was still not openly discussed or accepted. She felt strongly, however, that it was her mother's right to do as she liked. She also said that she was going to have a friend over for a sleepover and that the friend could ask what she wanted about her mother, but Melissa wasn't going to worry about it. A much more important issue was who would get Sally's attention. Sally herself felt pulled from both sides. The counsellor facilitated recognition of the legitimacy of Melissa's claim that her mother be there for her and that she have time alone with her; he also facilitated acknowledgement of the mother's right to have an intimate relationship. Another issue was Melissa's ability to choose when to participate in activities with Claire and when not to.

The last session included Claire, who had the ability to listen as well as to share. Although Melissa seemed more reserved than in other sessions she was able to say what most troubled her about the inclusion of Claire in the relationship. Melissa had felt she did not get enough attention from Sally even before she was involved with Claire. Sally would tend to become preoccupied, shut down and absorbed by television or other tasks. Claire felt free enough to say that this was an issue that troubled her as well. Sally smiled with pleasure at this common ground between her partner and her child, even at her own expense.

The counsellor, observing this conversation, did not tell himself that now any of these three persons would be free from frustration and loss as they try to figure out this complex relationship. He was glad that there was a flow of conversation and that difficult realities could be named. He was also aware that at 12 Melissa was at a vulnerable age, needing involved parents, needing adults who could put her first. Claire addressed Melissa directly about her desire to also be there for her and Melissa was cordial if not eager.

For an experienced counsellor a last session is never a time in which he may say that a family or couple's troubles are over. About this and other last sessions, he may say instead that something has been accomplished:

- a milestone was passed;
- a conversation could take place in which the difficulty of adding a new member to a family could be discussed without escalating into someone being wrong or someone being permanently excluded;
- one member of a family could own a limitation and give permission for that limitation to be discussed and dealt with; or
- a younger person could learn that she could speak about areas sensitive to her parent without losing that parent's love or attention.

Relational counselling may end without a formal final session

For many individual clients, counselling is an opportunity that they engage in for relief and end with reluctance. Frequently, they will take pains to include their counsellor in the ritual of their ending. Many families and couples end in a similar careful way – sometimes with gifts brought, letters written and a final session in which nothing much happens except the lingering of friends in an atmosphere of comfort and success. For many clients, however, relational counselling is a difficult achievement. Relationships are trouble; one cannot just explore and learn in safety at one's own pace. In relational counselling, clients encounter one another and are stretched in ways they cannot completely control. Even while they learn more about the nature of their relationships, they face the loss of a secure unquestioned stable point of view. In successful relationship counselling, clients are asked to integrate the roles of the counsellor – listening, understanding, reframing and restraining oneself – as well as to enjoy permission as clients to explore and express in their own way.

When some clients cancel abruptly without indication of improvement, the counsellor may speak to a supervisor about what she could have done differently and what part her own actions or lack of actions played in the termination of the counselling. In some cases of my own, I have clearly understood an excess of zeal on my part to bring about some change in one client in response to urgency felt from other clients or my own values overly stirred up. This has happened particularly in families in which there was apparent substance abuse. In other cases, in which a relationship was built around an 'emotional hierarchy' (Barrett, 1996) favouring one of its members, the opportunity for the 'secondary' family members to discover their own voices was intolerable to the person who held disproportionate power. Clients at the bottom end of the emotional hierarchy often return for individual counselling as they begin to disentangle from or change themselves within a relationship in which they were not able to be themselves.

Clients may also be quite positive and express commitment to the counselling when responding to a counsellor's follow-up, but still not return for another appointment. They may ask each other: 'Do you want to go again?' 'I don't know, do you want to go again?' 'Let's hold off for a month and see what happens'; or 'Things are going OK, let's wait and make an appointment when we need one'. They stopped because it had been good enough. A 'good enough' counselling helps a relationship move on its way. It would be lovely for the counsellor if the clients let him in on the ending of this useful work, but it is not his right and not the clients' obligation. Box 8.2 illustrates this kind of ending.

Box 8.2 'Oh we're fine for now, didn't you know that?'

The counsellor calls Sara Miller after the family had attended six sessions. He had already spoken to her son Tommy, who reported feeling 'pretty good' and told of some of his activities. Sara's initial concern was that Tommy, 17, had told his teacher that he 'sometimes didn't feel like living anymore'. As the counsellor met with Tommy and his two parents (an older brother had already moved out of the house and was not able to attend), a chronic problem emerged: his father, Tom Sr, was an admittedly heavy drinker and Sara was frequently furious with him and depressed about their marriage. After several meetings of Tommy and his parents and one meeting with Tommy alone and one with his parents alone, the family cancelled and did not reschedule.

> Sara: Oh, Charles! I've been meaning to get back to you. I'm glad you called . . . No I don't think we will be back, at least for a while . . . Tommy seems to have lost interest in the counselling. Tom and I have not been at each other's throats so much. As far as my worries about everyone in the family, I think I'm in remission!

In this case, I am delighted that Tommy has lost interest in the counselling. For a teenager, involved in his life, those words can mean the counselling has done its work. (If he lost interest while drifting away from contact with his parents and the activities of his age group, it would be a different matter.) Tommy was active in counselling when he was feeling lost and depressed, ashamed of his father and resentful of his mother. He wanted (and needed) counselling when his coming home was filled with dread; when he was burdened with responsibility in his role as middleman for his parents; when he was alone with his father after his father had been drinking and he was faced with the impossible alternatives of either silently tolerating lengthy alcohol-influenced lectures or of walking out on or otherwise insulting his father. After sessions in which his father admitted his alcohol problem; his mother admitted that dad's drinking or their marriage was not her son's responsibility; and both parents talked about their love for their son and their desire that he not build his life around them – his burdens dissolved. He and his father had talks with one another when his father was sober. In his presence (and his father's), his mother was able to talk of her admiration and love for her husband and that her anger at his drinking did not make that less true. Tommy was able to listen to some family stories about his parents' days before his arrival and their ideas about what the house would be like when he went away after high school graduation. Finally the three were able to discuss feelings about some of the dramatic scenes they all had suffered through over the past year. Tommy was able to express anger at his mother as well as his father for the tension he lived through. He had lost interest in family counselling because he had renewed interest in the regular concerns of a teenager's life.

Frequently, last sessions represent an end of a struggle

In a typical course of counselling, a couple may work for months in the aftermath of an affair by one partner. The conversation goes from anger to hurt to demands to pleading on the part of one partner. The experience may be one of defensiveness, shame, indignation, placating and compassion for the other.

For a person-centred relational counsellor, the task is to stay with both persons in all their complexity. This situation may seem impossible on the surface. One person can be absolute in her value that monogamy be unquestioned. She may feel that her husband's failure to be monogamous entitles her to unlimited reassurances and reparations. Her husband may be guilty as well as resentful of his partner's disturbing and (he fears) limitless anger. He may be ambivalent about the importance of monogamy, but incapable of speaking of this directly. In a safe atmosphere another reality can emerge. Two people can also find themselves talking about the unique bond they have together. They can talk about the history of the problems they have solved together: raising children; coping with work and money; helping one another grow up in relation to families of origin; and co-creating a place to live. In those realities there are bonds and intentions, not created by the counsellor, which can be resources to see them through their dilemmas. The counselling expands the conversation as seen in Box 8.3.

Box 8.3   An ending but not a guarantee

With one couple, Steve and Betsy, counselling was possible because of a connection and compatibility between them that was more resilient than a long secret affair that Steve had been in and a devastating consuming anger which Betsy suffered without apparent relief. The couple were stuck for three years in a cycle of anger and unsatisfying apology; suspicion and unconvincing reassurance. The counsellor worked in supervision to not become trapped in an agenda of trying to talk either of them into a different position (e.g. less anger and focus on Steve by Betsy; more disclosure, assertiveness and genuine understanding of Betsy's feelings by Steve).

The counsellor did encourage more talk about the story of their marriage; their relationship with their parents; their likes and dislikes and especially their here-and-now reactions to one another and to the events of their lives as individuals. He did not know whether they had enough to connect in the face of the whirlwind of energy around Steve's extramarital relationship and the possibility he would do it again. The counselling did not presume to answer that question for them even in unspoken assessment. In more than 18 months of counselling, every two weeks, Steve and Betsy managed a conversation which was complex and respectful intertwined with what Steve came to call the 'meeting of doom' – that combination of Betsy's most absolute anger and suspicion with Steve's unspoken hurt and spoken defensiveness.

The ending of the counselling was discussed for two months in advance. The last session was a celebration of the couple's ability to have conversations in the face of impossible predicaments. Each would prefer that the other was very different in important ways. Each enjoyed the other and the life he and she had very much and chose the life that they had made together. In the last session, the counsellor brought up what hadn't been resolved: it could not really be known whether Steve would have other affairs despite his insistence that he would not. It could not be known if Betsy could completely forgive him for the affairs he had had. It could not be known if Steve could handle Betsy's articulate and, to him, inexhaustible anger. It could not be known if Betsy could receive compassion from Steve without suspecting that he was just trying to placate her.

What was known was that each had touched the other in many ways that showed deep appreciation and affection. They knew how to have fun together; get things done together; have a sense of humour together; solve major financial setbacks together. It was known that each understood what it was like to grow up in the other's childhood home. Each knew the other could surprise him or her by unexpected understanding and compassion. Steve had been able to be angry with Betsy; and Betsy was able to understand that Steve could be angry with her without discounting her right to feel angry with him. Betsy could sometimes not give a damn whether Steve was monogamous or not; Steve could sometimes tell her some of the feelings which surrounded his affairs without seeming to justify them or blame them on Betsy.

Perhaps most importantly, the last session confirmed the relationship as one which depended consistently on many individual, unguaranteed choices by each of them. The counselling brought an end to the marriage as defined by a single issue talked about in a single way. It was a beginning of a relationship between more complex persons whose inclinations, opinions, needs and wants could no longer be taken for granted.

The educational aspect of counselling is made more explicit

In final sessions, says person-centred counsellor Bob Lee, the counselling has long since turned into a form of education. Bob makes his clients familiar with the key concepts of the person-centred approach. He makes sense out of his own behaviours using the term 'congruence' about his sharing of emotions which, sometimes unexpectedly, arose in family situations. He talks about getting down on the floor to be completely present for smaller children as a form of 'empathy'. He uses events in the course of the counselling to illustrate the effects of conditionality and unconditionality on the family encounters.

Similar to Bob, I use the term 'self-concept' and talk about it as something which can be fluid and open rather than rigid and closed. I apply it to the concrete events of the counselling. For example: 'How does your showing up at Joey's track meet with his forgotten sweatshirt fit in with your concept that you are a cold and distant father?'; or 'Wait a minute, I thought it was completely established that you, Mary, would never be the one who was more interested in making love? What was different for you on this occasion?'

Families and couples can learn the concept of the split between idealized self and self-concept. The counsellor can refer to this in her feedback to her clients. 'There is a better family somewhere that would always know how to say the right thing when facing something like this – how would they listen better than you two managed ten minutes ago?' Especially by the end of counselling, the counsellor has observed many moments of client behaviour which more than any lectures can help narrow the gap between what clients think they should be and who they are:

Fred, you just sat quietly and didn't interrupt once while Mary talked about feeling lonely and unsure. Did you notice yourself doing that?

It looks to me as though you just spent ten minutes negotiating about what to do about Alice's visit. Neither of you accused the other, diagnosed the other or raised your voice. Does that seem different to you? What is making it possible to talk to each other like this?

A major theme in last sessions is repeated focus on: 'What is different?' Awareness of changed behaviours allows clients to modify self-concept. Last sessions can be similar to final meetings of groups in which participants celebrate increased inner and interpersonal freedom. The counsellor, presumably long displaced from any pedestal, joins the couple and family in sharing observations about their increased congruence, empathy and acceptance. Like those of a group facilitator, her observations about the clients' own efforts are appreciated. If, throughout the counselling, she was facilitating change, now she is facilitating understanding and integrating change. She may encourage each family member to describe the most significant moment of the counselling and may describe the moment most significant to her:

> I was very moved how after that painful scene, *both* of you were quick to follow up and check on how the other was feeling. It seems as though both of you went from feeling very injured and very in the right to being undefensive and concerned about how the other felt.

Self-disclosure is a form of education that is highly compatible with the person-centred approach. In final sessions, the counsellor may speak about his own experiences in a family or in a couple with less risk of taking focus off the clients. Such self-disclosure may be particularly helpful in letting clients know that troubles and conflict do not end when (even helpful) counselling ends:

> I think that by the time I am 90, I will be patient enough to be the parent of a teenager. In the meantime, I am glad that my daughter feels free to call me on speaking to her loudly and indignantly before I have listened to her point of view.

> I don't know how my wife and I could manage without having some time alone just to talk at least once a week, if not every day or so.

The education that characterizes final sessions is, at best, person-centred, with clients as well as counsellors working to make useful sense out of their efforts and experiences:

> I realized that here he was, doing the very thing that I've been criticizing him for not doing, and I was shutting him off. So I said: 'OK, yes, I would like a cup of tea. Thank you.'

Before Geoff (a two-year-old) was born, Peggy and I used to always have time together just before bed to talk about her day; and sometimes I would brush her hair. We can't go back to those days – *she* wouldn't have the time even if *I* did! – but I'm going to go back to driving her to dance lessons again so that we at least have a little time together.

Final sessions sort out predicaments versus problems

In Chapter 5, I referred to the following concept, which is important in understanding the process of relational counselling:

> One of the most valuable lessons, among many valuable lessons, I learned from philosopher Abe Kaplan is to distinguish between a problem and a predicament. Problems can be solved; predicaments can only be coped with. Most of the affairs of life, particularly the most intimate and important ones such as marriage and child rearing, are complicated inescapable dilemmas – predicaments where no options look very good or better than any other. I believe that is true of management as well.
>
> A problem is created by something going wrong, by a mistake, defect, disease or a bad experience. When we find the cause we can correct it. A predicament, however, paradoxical as it may seem, is more likely to be created by conditions that we highly value. That is why we can only cope with it. (Farson, 1996: 42)

Counselling is most helpful when people finish with a shared sense of what problems they need to solve and what predicaments they need to endure. Ending sessions often involve an acknowledgement of what in their lives they can change and what they must learn to live with. During counselling, clients become free to say what they want and expect even while learning to tolerate the very different wants and needs of their significant others. Many behaviours change from this communication. One major change, however, is in the direction of acceptance. Behaviourist couples therapist Neal Jacobson's most recent research (Cordova et al., 1997) indicates that when members of a couple are able to understand and accept the other's difference from them, the effects of the therapy are more significantly lasting than through other means (see also Johnson and Greenberg, 1994b: 311–12, for reference to Rogers about this assertion). Rogers' 1961 statement seems very up to date:

> This tendency to react to any emotionally meaningful statement by forming an evaluation of it from our own point of view, is, I repeat, the major barrier to interpersonal communication . . . Real communication occurs and this evaluative tendency is avoided when we listen with understanding. What does this mean? It means to see the expressed idea

and attitude from the other person's point of view, to sense how it feels to him, to achieve his frame of reference in regard to the thing he is talking to. (Rogers, 1961b: 331–2)

The final sessions of counselling may contain client expression of their side of a predicament along with acceptance of the integrity and good will of another who takes another side. They are able to realize that two things may be true at the same time. For example, in early sessions a parent may yell at a counsellor that she cannot manage to be patient with one aspect of her handicapped daughter's behaviour. It is too much to ask. The counsellor, if she is wise, will agree with her or at least reflect back the feeling: 'It is too much to ask. It is not fair. It is more than I can do.' By the end of relational counselling she may also learn that *just because she cannot be patient doesn't mean that her daughter deserves or flourishes with impatience.* The end of counselling may be the beginning of her solving the problem of how to deal with her frustration and impatience without imposing it on her daughter. Here are two other examples:

- An extroverted, highly social woman realizes that she is entitled to want a companion who shares her love of closeness, involvement and social activities. Her husband, she realizes, is entitled to not like going out, to not like social scenes and to need large amounts of quiet time alone.
- A high school student is entitled not to like school and to be more interested in what her friends think about life than in her parents' expectations. Her parents are entitled to those expectations.

Coping with such predicaments is practical as well as existential. The very social woman can enjoy her husband at home and her friends outside. She may revive some of the lively things she did before she married, even while she remembers what she valued about her husband's introverted ways. He may learn how to be less defensive about his privacy and more appreciative of the liveliness he enjoyed when they first met. He may find ways he can tolerate some increase in social activities. A child can sometimes learn to endure the right amount of school his parents can tolerate rather than face the misery of their disapproval; his parents can give up their dream of an academically interested child. The student may start working harder to get them off his back or surprise himself and his parents with unexpected constructive energy. The parents may learn to notice and accept efforts the child is already making and remember the unconditional love they used to show before he was a teen. The parents of a handicapped child can learn to involve others in the care of their child; learn to trust that their child can deal with the fact that he has limited parents; and give up their ideal of a child who outgrows the need for care. Throughout person-centred relational counselling, the counsellor attempts neither to talk persons into acceptance of their lives as they are, nor to deny the contradictions and disappointments they must face. The process of counselling allows clients to learn how to live with this paradox. The beginning of counselling may look like this:

> *Client*: I don't know if I can live with someone who could have had an affair for over a year and kept it secret from me.
> *Counsellor*: You keep coming back to this. Can you accept a relationship with someone who has kept such a secret from you for so long?

Counselling with the same client may end looking like this:

> *Client*: The affair will never be over for me and I will never trust him in the same way again. What is different is that it is not the most important thing in our relationship anymore.

Box 8.4 is another example of the acceptance of a predicament.

Box 8.4   Your guilt is what is harming me today

David Sanders relates how, in a family living under the shadow of a disfiguring injury to a teenage girl when she was two, the parents' guilt and mutual blame over the incident continued to haunt the child 12 years later. For this teenager, her parents' unresolved feelings made the reconstructive and cosmetic operations she frequently had to live through be about something very wrong about her, rather than simply part of the business of her particular life. They were stuck still struggling with which of them was more to blame for her injury, without realizing that their tension was translated by their daughter as their inability to accept her. She was near suicidal. Her parents 'had blinders on'. They were just focused on the next operation rather than on the meaning it might have for her. The goal of the therapy became her parents accepting what had happened and giving up the restless search for blame. For the sake of their daughter, the parents had to learn to forgive themselves and each other for an incident that neither had wanted to happen. The learning took place through focus on listening to their daughter in the present.

In the last session in relational counselling, acceptance of predicaments is celebrated. Each client must accept the difference between what he thinks should be true and what is. In the paradoxical logic of both person-centred theory *and* systems theory, acceptance by one person often facilitates change in the other. A woman may accept grief that something seems to remain stubbornly true – her mother and her husband do not enjoy each other. A man may give up trying to be in charge of something that never belonged to him to begin with – his wife's weight. A client may agree to the termination of a bad agreement – a new stepfather is not a party to the 'raising' of his wife's 14-year-old son. The counsellor confirms these 'passive' achievements as just as difficult as active achievements: 'How were you able to stay out of that argument the other night? How were you able to know you could love Arlene while not trying to take charge of her son's behaviours?' Final sessions may celebrate both that one client has become more active and responsible – e.g. Fred has met with his teacher and worked out their differences – and that his counterpart is no longer rescuing him – e.g. Fred's mother has *not* met with his teacher for him.

CHAPTER 9

Couples Counselling

Since many person-centred counsellors may have more opportunity to see couples than families, in this chapter I will reflect on the experience of working with couples. (See Box 9.1 for some of Carl Rogers' reflections on couples.) Couples counselling may be easier than counselling with larger family groups, since couples with children are able to focus on self and the other without the additional pressure of the role and responsibilities of parent. In couples counselling everyone is a peer, at least theoretically. Couples counselling, however, has its own unique challenges. Usually, the counsellor must deal with sharing the same gender socialization as only one member of the couple. Sometimes counselling concentrated on the quality of a relationship can stir strong and very personal emotions about what is missing and wanted from one's whole life, not just the relationship. Couples counselling is not only concerned with the particular conflicts within an individual couple, but frequently involves the nature of relationship as each has separately come to define it. Working with cognitive as well as affective material, the counsellor is partly facilitator, partly witness and partly educator.

What is different for a counsellor when she sees a couple rather than an individual? In the first sessions, she is challenged to create an atmosphere in which *both* clients learn that they can speak and be heard. Early couples work is similar to the beginning of a group, in that participants must learn to trust and gradually give up layers of superficial positioning, positive and negative, in order to get to their most important truths. It is also quite different from a group, in that the counsellor will usually need to be somewhat active and creative in order to assist *each client to get into the conversation without driving the other one out*. In couples counselling I have found that almost all empathy is idiosyncratic (see Bozarth, 1984).

Box 9.1   Carl Rogers and couples counselling

In *Becoming Partners* (1972a), Carl Rogers presented his reflections based on his long experience as a researcher, interviews with several couples, and his own marriage of more than 50 years. He found four threads that seemed central in the lives of couples who had managed to have a successful relationship:

1. *Commitment*: which he described, after careful thought, as 'working together on the changing process of our relationship, because that relationship is currently enriching our love and our life and we wish it to grow.' (201)
2. *Communication*: which includes sharing any 'persistent feeling' as well as a commitment to bring all one's ability to understand to the other's shared thoughts and feelings. (204)
3. *Dissolution of roles*: a freedom to live by one's own choices rather than by expectations and 'by the wishes, the rules, the roles which others are all too eager to thrust upon us.' (206)
4. *Becoming a separate self*: which includes discovery of self, experiencing one's own values and encouragement of growth for both. (206–9)

Although Rogers did not address couples therapy specifically, he was concerned about how little research was devoted to successful couples relationships. He was particularly convinced that if people learned to understand and befriend their own and others feelings at an early age, the quality of their committed relationships would greatly improve (216). Twenty-three years later, in a recent review of outcome research in marital therapy, it was noted that couples who respond better to marital therapy 'do not have premature closure in their problem-solving attempts and are less distressed at the beginning of therapy, younger, more emotionally engaged with each other (i.e. have not emotionally disengaged from the relationship), less rigid in their gender roles and not depressed' (Bray and Jouriles, 1995: 467). This picture confirms Rogers' sense of a better chance of success for those persons who are less locked into a self-defeating style and who have certain pre-existing attitudes to bring into the building of a relationship. 'Younger', in my mind, can refer to a way of being rather than a chronological age. When Carl Rogers was a boy, it was predicted that he 'would die young'. In his later years, travelling all over the world for challenging projects, Rogers liked to say that the prediction was right: 'I will die young' (Kirschenbaum, 1979: 433).

Elements of person-centred couples counselling

Person-centred couples counselling contains elements of *curiosity*, of *a philosophy about relationships*, of *letting go*, of *confrontation at the same time as acceptance*, of *empathic understanding for each individual* and of *active facilitation of dialogue*.

Curiosity

The counsellor is nothing if not a witness to the complexity and uniqueness of each relationship. Members of a couple themselves may feel under the shadow of a bland, meaningless, predictable existence. In the counselling experience, they can view themselves and their relationship with a fresh perspective. For the counsellor, their being together is a new story. She may relate to the couple in a variety of ways, but the interest in the narrative of how they got together, and what they *thought* a relationship *should* be is irreplaceable, whether expressed in careful reflective listening or active questioning. In the presence of a counsellor who is meeting their partner with the interest, respect and attention which they once brought to the relationship, some indifferent, out-of-love, self-justifying, brooding people may recover their sense of humour, if not appreciation for their relationships.

A philosophy about relationships

The counsellor is present not only with her skills as a facilitator, but also as a person with an approach to counselling, with her own perspective on relationship and experiences (good or bad) in relationship. Sometimes saying nothing is exactly congruent with the needs of a couple and sometimes personal stories, answers to questions, or sharing of a philosophy are the only ways to be truly present to a couple working on their own relationship.

Letting go

After a working atmosphere has been established, the counsellor's task is to facilitate a direction that only the clients can establish. In terms of process, a couple may seek the non-interference which allows them to work safely in their own way; they may also direct the counsellor to be involved and share perspective on their interaction. The counsellor may prefer, personally, that a couple stays together, or that one member of the couple would make more efforts to be responsive to the needs of the other. She is disciplined, however, to look for how a particular couple will find their own responses to a dilemma. One person's withholding may serve a purpose that no one could guess. Another person's anger may help achieve balance that could not be foreseen.

I must admit that I have a natural tendency to help couples that come together for counselling stay together after counselling. Nevertheless, it is my job as counsellor not to overtly or covertly impose this inclination on a couple. I feel equally strongly that any counsellor whose personal experience was enhanced by divorce be aware of and deal with potential bias rather than assume it would be helpful for a couple. The counsellor must beware 'prior knowledge' (Anderson, 1997) about what a couple should or should not do. Similarly, she must beware assumptions about a couple's compatibility. The chance of 'success' between persons who love each other can look pretty dismal at certain points in their life.

Confrontation at the same time as acceptance

Successful counselling influences clients to see their own thoughts and behaviours as part of the dynamic which creates their partner's thoughts and behaviours. If I act *'as if'* my partner dislikes me, doesn't respect me, is fundamentally selfish or does not have good intentions, then all my actions will reflect that perspective and help create what I fear (Stuart, 1980). The counsellor may explicitly discuss this common factor in human relationships. More frequently, he may reflect the incongruence between what one partner says and does and the other perceives. For example:

> *Counsellor*: You told him about the affair then because you wanted him to know how desperate you had become about the lack of closeness between you. Is that right? Phil, what did you hear?
> *Phil*: That she was through with me and wanted a divorce.
> *Counsellor*: What are you hearing now and seeing as we have this conversation?

The counsellor reflects, but does not argue, because the client may have a need to maintain a rigid misperception until she is ready to let it go. 'It finally occurred to me that "there may be some truth in that",' one client said of her partner's long-contested explanation for one of his idiosyncrasies. It had taken several months of intense dialogue in counselling before she could say that.

Empathic understanding for each individual

The counsellor's capacity to understand each member of a couple adds a dimension that the couple locked in one dreary segment of their reality may find renewing. The counsellor can meet each member of a couple as a person who works, plays, has opinions and has dimensions other than his or her role in the marriage. Couples counselling often includes elements of individual counselling with the partner present (see Mearns, 1994b: 57–8). This usually happens after trust is well established and should be undertaken only if both clients are capable of personal exploration *and* of standing by while the other works on individual issues. (The counsellor must beware of designating one person as the perpetual client and the other as co-counsellor.)

Active facilitation of dialogue

A theme of this book is that the relational counsellor has a responsibility for the setting in which relationship work takes place. Sometimes the clients have a compatible understanding of the tasks of counselling. With some couples, a nod of the head starts off a lively and evenly distributed sharing in which the counsellor is needed only as witness. For others, it is enormously important that the counsellor be active so that *both* clients can speak, listen, respond to what the other said, and listen again. The counsellor also has a role in clarifying the contract of the counselling. For example, a member of a couple may come in and act as if he is in individual counselling and initiate a depressed or angry monologue. The counsellor listens carefully *and* makes room for the other's response. Box 9.2 gives an example of an extended dialogue in a counsellor's office.

Box 9.2   Facilitating a dialogue

Bill and Tony came to me for counselling every two weeks for nine months, then returned for a series of four or five sessions once a year for three years. The counselling was about the mixture of good and bad in their lives; their differences and their similarities; their values and their dreams; and their comfort with being a couple. I learned about them both and actively shared my perspectives about their individual journeys, as well as their life as a couple. I communicated my understanding that they had fundamental values in common, despite their obvious differences in social comfort and choices about use of free time. In many of our sessions, I was simply a mediator, allowing both sides of sensitive issues to be thoroughly clarified. My efforts to empathically track and confirm each person's thought process was central to the counselling. The attitudes that seemed most important in the counselling were:

I would provide permission to suspend final decisions so that any possibility could be discussed without threat. A third party who is calm in the middle of urgent, competing views can facilitate dialogue about subjects that could otherwise provoke demands and counter-demands. For example, when Bill said it was really time for him to leave town and return to the mountains of Arizona, even though Tony was intensely involved with a local social service agency, my presence allowed them exploratory conversation rather than any rush toward either/or decision-making. Bill, it turned out, needed to speak about his readiness to be back in the mountains where there was a chance for a complete change in work and where he could climb and otherwise live a simpler, more outdoor life. He wanted to pretend Tony was not in his life so that he could hear his own voice. Within the setting of counselling, Tony was more receptive than expected. He was eager, in fact, to hear Bill talking more from his heart about what mattered to him. He didn't rule out the possibility that, if Bill wished him to move, the mountains might be a welcome relief from the stress of his current job. Though they did not move, it was important for each to feel safe in talking about his widest vision for himself without the other feeling threatened and defensive.

I would not see any problem as meaning that one of them was right and the other was wrong. One issue dominating their attention was the great unevenness with which they worked at renovating their house. The counselling office could be full of Bill's frustration and resentment that he shouldered most of the work, about commitments not fulfilled, about feeling foolish in his seemingly one-sided devotion to what he had thought was a common project. Without denying Bill's experience, Tony could admit that he did not care as much about the house as Bill. He would much rather Bill would do less than have to live with Bill's unhappiness at working alone. In addition, Tony felt that he tried to make other contributions to their common enterprises rather than work on the house. Finally, Tony was, gradually, even becoming more naturally attached to craftsmanlike work on the house rather than a grudging subordinate trying to improve his habits. It is an achievement of counselling that strong contradicting opinions can be laid side by side with neither one diminished nor refuted.

I would not take on the job of facilitating equal justification for both partners. Sometimes couples are very unequal in what they contribute; and only the words 'I'm sorry', or 'I appreciate what you do', or 'What do I need to do to make up for it?' or other similarly nondefensive responses have any meaning. For example, only with an extra lifetime could Tony ever catch up with Bill in quantity (and especially quality) of work on their house. Frequently, a relational ledger cannot be balanced by action, but only by understanding and forgiveness (see Boszormenyi-Nagy et al., 1991: 163–5, for his discussion of the family ledger).

I would provide safety for strong emotions to be expressed without becoming rigid positions. I attempted to hear the full content and meaning of each person's words, making space for meanings to be thoroughly understood, rather than ground under the feet of heavy, urgent attempts to persuade. Both of these men were good at active listening and at empathic connection with the other. At times of high emotionality, however (when as with most couples, topics included money, sex, time spent together and other people in their lives), they were unable to hear the other's voice without feeling either a judgement or a demand. The counsellor is a representative for the space in between – the time in which each person can hear one person's truth before it is driven out by the other's very different position. Coming to the counselling meant, in part, a choice in favour of that space and an admission that in this stage of the relationship it was not possible.

Counsellor variation between teaching and facilitation

Relationship counselling involves dialogue, not only between members of a couple, but within the counsellor, about different aspects of her role. The couples counsellor is asked to be both responsive in the here and now to whatever clients bring and a resource familiar with the troubles and opportunities of a couples relationship. I consider it important to be ready to give clients information and especially to ask questions which may open awareness of the more objective dimensions of relationships. I am also aware that information, advice and expectations are available everywhere and that a couple comes seeking counselling in which they feel they can be met and taken seriously as persons. Some counsellors maintain that skills training is the most important element of couples work (Stuart, 1980; Bray and Jouriles, 1995). Box 9.3 discusses a skills-oriented approach which its founder, Bernard Guerney, considers to be based on the person-centred approach (1984).

Box 9.3   The relationship enhancement approach of Bernard Guerney

Mary Helen Snyder (1989) wrote a description of the 'Relationship Enhancement Model of Couple Therapy' of Bernard Guerney. 'Since Rogers was not at all averse to training therapists in the skills of person-centered therapy, I am not certain that he would have disagreed with Guerney's perception that people would not automatically develop these skills as a result of being adequately understood themselves' (360). Guerney's relationship enhancement work is a structured way of teaching and directing client interactions in which congruence is safe, empathy is modelled, and acceptance is made possible by the counsellor's active reduction of opportunities for threat or defence.

Paraphrasing Snyder, relationship enhancement (RE) approach includes:

- Skills training for which the primary method is demonstration and modelling.
- Emphasis on coaching to see the world as the other sees it. Snyder emphasizes this, comparing it, after Bateson (1979), with the more complete vision given by having two eyes rather than one. In so far as a partner learns to see the world from his partner's point of view as well as from his own, so is that person able to have a clearer vision of the relationship.
- Facilitation of structured dialogue to make possible full communication that allows the conditions of the person-centred approach to flourish. Particularly important is learning how to express your feelings and needs in such a way that your partner does not hear them as an attack on or rejection of her. Similarly the skill of empathy as learned in RE includes focusing on grasping the experience of one's partner to such an extent that rebuttal and defensiveness become irrelevant.
- A structure that is like 'a scaffolding that carefully supports the person-centered processes of treating each other congruently, empathically and with unconditional positive regard . . .' (Snyder, 1989: 368)

In my own work I have often used Guerney's application of the psychodrama technique of 'doubling' to facilitate client communication during moments of extreme crisis or for clients who are almost unable to speak without accusation, personalized criticism or contempt. The counsellor simply listens to one client well enough to grasp what they are trying to communicate. Then, with the client's permission and with the client asked to correct any inaccuracies, the counsellor speaks as the client to their partner, conveying the emotional heart of the communication and leaving out the provocative attacking style. Initially this provides a way for couples to bring up 'impossible issues' without being flooded with anxiety and rage (see Snyder, 1989: 369–70, for an example of this).

For further understanding of this approach to work with couples, the reader may consult Snyder's article in the *Person Centered Review* (1989), Bernard Guerney's article in *Client-Centered Therapy and The*

> *Person-Centered Approach* (Levant and Shlien, 1984) or Bernard
> Guerney's many works on relationship enhancement with couples (for
> example, 1994). Barrett-Lennard (1998) also discusses this approach
> in his excellent review of the literature of person-centred family and
> couples work.

Sometimes feedback may help a client regain a sense of perspective. Carl Rogers once humorously described how rigidly members of a couple can cut themselves off from communication by certain types of thinking.

> It is as if they are saying: 'I am correct and accurate and sound in my view
> of the situation, my perception of its elements, my interpretation of its
> meaning. My view is the right and true one. You are unfortunately
> mistaken and inaccurate in your view of the situation and in your analysis
> of what it means. Your view is false and wrong, yet you stubbornly hold
> to it.
>
> 'I am honest and straightforward and fundamentally good in my
> approach to our relationship and its problems. Unfortunately, you are
> none of these things. You are essentially bad and evil and untrustworthy
> in your approach to the whole situation. My motives are good. Yours are
> not.'

Try reading the above aloud to a significant other! Without the participation of the counsellor, members of a couple may drive each other away by an attitude or tone of which they are not aware. On the other hand, a client may be able to preach, be self-righteous and absolutely one-sided in order to work through a past hurt if the counsellor provides the expectation of a fair chance to be also heard for her partner. Feeling heard by the counsellor and her partner, an angry client may make herself ready to hear another side. One client, for example, kept returning to recitation of how injured she was by a separation her husband had initiated years before. This injury came up in three different sessions, no matter what our topic. By the fourth session, she had softened considerably, was non-defensive in hearing his side of the story and was ready to re-commit to the relationship.

As I listen to each member of a couple's own statement of what brings them in, how they suffer, what they want, what their story of the relationship is and how they interact with their partner, I am mostly there as a facilitator. However, as an experienced teacher and reader of research literature on successful relationships, I know that behaviour matters; that environmental and developmental events impinge upon subjective perception; that frame of reference determines the nature of events.

For some couples I see, there are opportunities to suggest workbook exercises oriented toward reflection on and written and spoken expression of one's preferred way of communicating, allocating responsibilities and resolving conflict (Stuart and Jacobson, 1987). Their responses can help provide a framework for discussions based on information rather than on assumptions derived from their frustrations. Some couples are most at home in a learning atmosphere in which work on skills is part of their expectations. Other couples, however, give clear signals that they simply need the counsellor to be there with them in their process and any talk of workbooks would be a disturbing interference. In Box 9.4, facilitation, teaching and personal involvement are each important in response to client expression of anger in couples work.

Box 9.4 Anger in couples work

Just as he can't get away from it in life, the counsellor must deal with a variety of challenges regarding anger in couples work. First, he must be aware that some clients may be so intensely angry that any reframing, learning exercises or role play would be an affront. For example, one woman client recently became very aware of a long-suppressed, low-grade anger that had taken on a new strong life of its own. Her feelings had become unpredictable, but were certainly no longer subject to any attempts to modify or channel them. She wanted her relationship; she wanted counselling to find a way to reconnect. She didn't feel like any programme of self-improvement; she simply wanted to see what the conversation would bring. She was only able to tolerate the minimum requirement of couples counselling: that the counsellor would listen to her partner as well as to her. The non-anxious presence of the counsellor allowed her partner to tolerate her anger with less need to retreat in defensiveness.

Sometimes, however, members of a couple will have such a way of dealing with anger that it would be confusing and inauthentic not to encourage reflection on it. They will habitually threaten divorce; they will shout in the other's face; they will bring up sensitive matters at the time when the other is most likely to be threatened; they will call names and accuse the other of the precise inadequacies that person most fears. They might habitually confront a morning person late at night; and a night person just as she is getting up. Couples can fall into the trance-like sense that their relationship is infinitely immune from the effects of their behaviour. The counsellor is not in charge of training in etiquette and is certainly not the judge of a couple's way of being. He can, however, raise questions about the incongruence between what a couple intend – to resolve their differences and restore intimacy – and how they behave – as though the other were not deserving of respect. The following is an example of an inelegant but heartfelt confrontation.

> One lively couple, Gail and Fred, asked for the counsellor's full involvement from the outset. 'Don't give me any of that non-directive bullshit,' was Gail's gentle invitation for engagement. The counsellor refereed, advocated for equal time, lent his voice to express strong feelings as they existed underneath strident accusations; and was humbly silent as once or more in the hour each member of the couple would say something that was their direct experience rather than their adversarial position.
>
> The couple were stretched by an accumulation of marriage events, children, complete job changes, growing a decade-and-a-half older, and time deprivation because of work and school. Sometimes the office could barely hold the sharp, intense feelings which tended to be expressed as absolute truths rather than individual feelings.
>
> Finally Gail demanded intensely that the counsellor give his opinion about whether or not it would be worthwhile to continue, not only the counselling, but the relationship itself. He had heard how bad it was, how hurt they were, how let down they were. 'Will you tell us,' she yelled, 'if there is any reason why we shouldn't give this up?' The counsellor answered, warned by a murderous look away from the conventional 'It's really not for me to say', or 'What do *you* think?' He said, 'I would be likely to have doubts about your relationship continuing if it had ever been tried with *either* of you showing *any trace* of using even *minimal social skills* in your conversations with each other. I have no idea what might happen if you did.'
>
> When the couple returned two weeks later, against all predictions, and were in fact getting along better than they had in weeks, the counsellor asked what was different. 'Skills!' said Gail. The counsellor's challenge was, in the circumstances, a way of showing regard for the couple. It was, in the give-and-take of the session, both critical of their behaviour and unlimited in openness to what they might become.

I often recommend that clients attend one of many workshops available for couples in which communication, conflict resolution, methods for sharing responsibility and authority are experientially taught (Lebow, 1997). One important element in education programmes is exposure to other couples. Seeing how issues come up in other partnerships can take the feeling of personal attack or inadequacy out of one's own relationship.

However, if my counselling consisted only of the rote application of methods to the couple's problems or of teaching a way of being in a relationship, few of the couples I see would remain in the office with me after a first session. The heart of good couples counselling is the facilitation of each person's story and their partner's listening to that story. The counsellor must be a trustworthy person with whom the client can not only share his story, but can also take risks for change either in the direction of assertiveness or receptivity. 'I come here because it's the only place I know we are going to talk,' is how one person put it.

The following case example illustrates the blending of teaching and facilitation, as well as many of the elements of person-centred couples counselling discussed above:

> A couple came to see me who had been married for over 15 years, having started their relationship when they were in their early teens, then having married in their early twenties after a separation. They had one much loved child. As is frequently the case, the wife, Mary, initiated the counselling. Rob, the husband, came in reluctantly, almost as angry at his wife for insisting on the counselling when they 'could just work it out [them]selves' as he was at her for involving his parents to the point that they were calling him to make sure he was all right. Depressed over the loss of one long-lasting, satisfying job and stuck in a good-paying job which he found taxing and uninteresting, Rob was withdrawn from his wife and child; while Mary was increasingly critical, negative and full of threats to leave if he was not going to be a more active husband to her.
>
> Having a counsellor was helpful because he was able to be someone to whom Rob would talk and someone Mary could trust enough to suspend her urgent need to express her pent-up feelings long enough for Rob to talk. As in many couples sessions, it was important to make sense out of the great rift that had grown between the couple. The counsellor was empathic with Rob's reasons to be on the couch watching every televised sport in existence as well as Mary's reasons to feel that she must sound a loud and persistent alarm. He showed acceptance of Rob's avoidance as well as Mary's urgency. The counsellor also let the couple know that Mary's critical talking and Rob's ignoring her were similar to many couples' reactions to a relationship that has become painful.
>
> The counsellor was interested in the way that Rob started feeling bad about his work, his weight and his health; and in his inclination to keep his feelings to himself the worse things felt. Rob avoided Mary not only because of his desire to hide his sense of loss and dislike of the progress of his life; but also because even a few words of his on many topics would unleash a flood of words of sympathy, as well as definite plans to do something about his predicament. As happens in many couples, depression for one partner can lead him to a defensive, avoiding posture. This can draw out a sometimes overwhelming expression of worry and hurt in the other, which in turn increases the withdrawn position of the first.
>
> The counsellor also listened to Mary, who was a long way down a road of grief, loss and anger that Rob, self-preoccupied, could not hear. As each person's trouble in the relationship was heard and confirmed, another story emerged, which they started telling together. They told about how they first fell in love – why when they were older they had needed to break up and live separately – why they got back together. 'I just couldn't

find anybody that I loved like Mary,' said Rob. They also told about what they had been through together about money, about raising a lively daughter, about their difficult parents, one of whom was often highly involved in their relationship.

In a sense the couples counsellor is a participant in a research project, joining a couple in assessing the way their feelings are the result of, or the cause of, the conditions of the relationship. In the case described above, the counsellor said, among other things:

- I understand that you did not want to come, Rob.
- It's Rob's turn, Mary.
- Did you know that in research on hundreds of American couples it was found that males are much more physically distressed by angry, emotional confrontation than are females? The same research also showed that females are much more physically distressed by being ignored or otherwise shut out? Does that sound like you?
- Did you also have some feelings at the time that Rob found out that his job at the airport service centre was being discontinued?
- It sounds like a lot of things are happening with you when you lie on that couch alone watching football.

The counselling lasted five sessions. On the fifth they brought a gift for the counsellor; and his only job was to make sure that *Mary* received some vestige of equal time as they talked about new kinds of conversation they were now having.

CHAPTER 10

One Family's Experience

I interviewed the Clark family recently about their life together and their experiences in counselling. I had met with them, individually and as a group, 25 times over a period of two years and seven months. At the beginning of our sessions, almost three years ago, Jenny was 38, a divorced working mother, Zack was 16 and Matt was 12.

The family asked for my help because Matt had been frequently suspended from school and was not turning in his homework, and because his mother felt he had 'low self-esteem'. Jenny had divorced Zack and Matt's father, Rick, while she was pregnant with Matt. Alcoholic, frequently unemployed, and sometimes living on the street, he lived as a variably difficult presence on the edges of their life. He had called the boys, sometimes only Zack, and invited them to do things with him inconsistently throughout their lives; had almost never contributed to their support and would turn up or disappear unpredictably. When I met them, the boys had stories about his embarrassing, unplanned ways of doing things when he was with them. They sometimes heard promises about things he would do with them that would remain promises. Jenny, as often happens with the custodial parent, would be torn between her own anger at him and her desire to ensure the boys have a chance at enjoying a father they could respect. 'I can't lie about him to them,' she once said, 'I try not to interfere with their relationship with him. When he promises something and doesn't show up, I try to make excuses for him and try not to say anything bad about him, but I'm mad too because he disappointed them again.'

When I first met with the family Jenny was concerned with the effects on Matt of his father's particular way of being with him. Having left the family before Matt was born, Rick would for years relate only to his eldest son; he would plan outings for Zack in which Matt was not included. Jenny would sometimes intervene, but was not able to prevent a situation in which Matt was a kid without even an absent father.

Jenny was concerned about Matt's self-image. He spoke around the house in ways that to her indicated he did not feel worth much. His work in school was considerably below his potential; and a particular problem was his not turning in his homework. He would sometimes complete it and not turn it in.

What are the boundaries of a family?

A major question in relational counselling is: who should attend? Family therapists, particularly structural family therapists, would strongly urge that an absent father or mother be included if possible. It is often helpful for an estranged parent to come to sessions, either with their children, alone or even with their ex-spouse. Such a meeting can bring in new information about a missing member, affirm permission for children to accept and enjoy both parents without hurting either, and invite new possibilities in the development of family and individual self-concept.

I suggested that I invite Rick to some of the sessions. Matt especially, definitely did not want him to attend. 'If he comes, I don't', was his succinct way of putting it. Jenny was also not enthusiastic, but said she would go along if I really wanted to get him to come. In other cases I have been fairly assertive – especially when there was a father involved with his children, but estranged from their mother. I met the Clarks on their terms. Convinced that their understanding of his story would influence the story of their lives, I still raised many questions about their father and ex-husband. In our interview, they indicated without enthusiasm that my questions were necessary and may have been helpful:

> *In our interview, Zack described the effects of the father's absence*: Personally I think it's made us all a lot stronger. I mean, my mom . . . I don't know anyone else who could do that [support and raise kids by herself] . . . We had to get out there and learn things on our own. It has made us all more independent.
>
> *His mother said*: They just have to take the initiative. No one is there to say 'get on with your homework'.
>
> *Zack discussed how he handled their father's inconsistent, often difficult presence in their life*: If I was anybody else I would probably not have anything to do with the guy, but I just can't do it. I'm too forgiving a person to shut anybody completely out of my life. I don't think I could ever do what he's done to me. Not being there. Not giving me a cent for 16 years. I would never do anything that bad to him. Even if it just meant not contacting him or being a downright jerk to him. I believe people should have a second chance to be good. I know that my dad has a good heart inside of him. I know he could still make something out of himself. He better do it pretty soon because he probably doesn't have much time because of drugs and stuff. [Later] Stuff like that nobody should do to anyone. I just can't *not* forgive him.
>
> *I say*: Does that have an effect on your own feelings?
>
> *Zack*: Yeah! It makes me feel like a strong person. [At 18 Zack is working on his concept of the father in his life and in doing so is shaping his own self-concept.]

Matt, younger, his eyes full of thoughts, denying that he has much to say, only adds this: I just don't really like my dad. I don't have any anger. I just don't like him.

Matt had earlier reported that he had been having more contact with his father. His father had been reaching out more to him than in the past and for years had been calling and speaking to Matt as well as to Zack. Over the time of our counselling Matt has come to expect two things of me: that I will bring up the subject of his father and that I will not push it. When Zack is present, Matt will sometimes bring up the subject himself in the form of stories about what their father has done lately.

I think two things: first, that Matt is resilient and that he and his family have figured out how to have a life without Rick being very central or reliable; second, that making sense out of Rick's story will create more possibilities for Matt. With their mother present, I have sometimes asked questions like: 'How do we know that your lives will turn out differently from your father's?' My intention, in order to deal with it constructively, is to make explicit a worry that I feel has been implicit in the family thinking. Other questions have included: 'What about Rick led Jenny to fall in love with him?'; 'At one point, why did he seem to turn away from a life of active involvement with his boys?'; and 'Under what circumstances, even now, could Rick's life be different?'

The counsellor is in psychological contact with the client

From the beginning, my task with Matt was complex. His brother and mother were very articulate and able to say what they wanted directly from the counselling and in other areas of their life. When Matt was alone with me, he was humorous but taciturn. He answered questions just enough, however, to give me the feeling that he was processing in complex and interesting ways, but was not ready perhaps this year and for several years to communicate with the easy flow of words that characterized his mother and brother. Over the years I have known him, just when I was about to say that we should do him a favour and no longer encourage counselling, he would say, in effect, don't stop: 'It would not be entirely boring to meet a few more times'. In individual meetings with Matt I would do much of the talking. I was a scavenger who from words, stories and other signs of personality was putting together a sculpture of a person who is perhaps as sensitive as his mother and as intelligent as his brother, but who is not yet ready to directly say what is on his mind.

When his brother was present Matt was most at ease and would tell vivid entertaining stories of family life and of the foibles of others. He remembered all the details of Zack, his mom and his life, and anything I would tell him of my own family. In earliest family meetings he was court jester and raconteur about his brother's adventures and misadventures. In our last sessions he was insightful and persistent about fairness in the family and how life was changing as Zack moved out more on his own. Then and now he can be seen – animated, involved and intelligent – but only if you do not focus your gaze directly on him.

When I met with Matt and his mother as a pair, I often tried to ask her questions about her life and family rather than have the conversation just be about Matt's difficulties. We talked about her growing-up family; her early years with Rick and why she had chosen him to begin with; her assessment of what Zack and Matt's father was like at Matt's age. Matt would participate with questions, commentary and, of course, humour. In general we limited time with the two of them because it was hard to get away from the trap of two talkative adults, Jenny and me, bearing down on the one kid.

About our family meetings, Zack said:

> I think mainly it just cracked open a lot of subjects that we never talked about. It helped us all get across points toward each other that we felt in a controlled environment instead of being at home or whatever and trying to describe what you felt to people. Because at home it is more like *telling* somebody – you are kind of putting your feelings onto somebody, whereas here it's more open.

The clients are in a state of incongruence

The reason his mother initiated the counselling was to build up Matt's self-esteem. One approach to this would be to help him do better at school and other activities so that he could have greater grounds for positive self-evaluation. Such an agenda is tempting for counsellor as well as client – and it sometimes works! A family, however, must be careful about a programme of good ideas intended to make another family member feel good about himself. They may, without knowing it, cross a boundary into criticizing him for *not* doing the things that make him feel *good* about himself in such a way that he feels *bad* about himself! This may be the most common incongruence of the most well intentioned families, my own included.

In family sessions it was therefore very easy to get into a lengthy session of 'what's wrong with Matt?'. Zack, two years older than Matt and very committed to school work and other achievements, found it hard to understand why Matt did not try harder in this area. Jenny, hard-working and eager for both boys to succeed, was frustrated by what she saw as Matt's refusal to do very simple things which would make his life easier. When I interviewed the family, Jenny reminded me of a session that had been among the most important for her:

> That time you had Zack and I go out to the hall and write down what was good about Matt. It made me think that I have to start building him up. There we were – both of us weren't able to think about anything good about him. We know they are there [the good things], but he's so inside himself, you wouldn't even notice if [something] was good. He flaunts . . . his bad side.
>
> We did come up with things after a while, but how hard it was made me sick to my stomach. I went home and prayed and prayed that I would think about good things about him. I worked on it.

I remembered that session. It was a session in which I was feeling desperate with the sense that we were doing the opposite of what any of us had intended. This feeling may be the sign that someone is meeting the incongruence that is at the heart of a family's trouble. I knew we were caught in a deteriorating relationship (Rogers, 1959). *What would you, the reader, have done?* Would you have sat next to Matt and expressed your guess at what it felt like to be criticized? (A good idea! Why didn't I think of it at the time?) Would you have said: 'I feel angry and frustrated. I thought we were meeting to help Matt, but it looks like all that we can think to do is criticize him.' (This is what I would say now, I think, because of the relationship of mutual trust that now exists between the family and me – especially since Matt would more likely join the conversation. I probably could have said it then. In *that* moment, however, I had the concern that such a statement would have led to more talk *about* Matt *around* Matt, but *not including* Matt.) I asked, instead, if Zack and Mom would leave the room to do the task described above, while I would just tune in to Matt by himself. Matt's mother, in any event, took the session as her opportunity to see the discrepancy between what she intended and thought she was doing – helping Matt to have higher self-esteem – and what she was in fact doing – joining Zack in a barrage of criticism.

Earlier in our review interview, I had asked Jenny what gave her hope about her boys. Right away, she had answered about Matt 'I think he's very smart. He has a good mind. He has his own opinions and he's not going to let anyone railroad him. And he's got a very good heart.'

'You didn't take long to answer,' I said. 'I've been working on it,' she said.

The counsellor is congruent

In my last counselling session with this family, it was easy to be congruent in that I felt that they knew me and trusted me well enough so that I could be myself. I was blunt and humorous with them; we made fun of each other. I asked with concern about their lives and was both a friend *and* a professional. They seemed to have come as much to show how they were processing their problems as to talk about what was wrong. The boys were 15 and 18 rather than 12 and 15; and they had known me for two-and-a-half years. It was easy for me to respect and feel respected. We had been through many events together.

During earlier sessions, I was alert and attentive, less to my own internal processing than to the job of figuring out how two lively boys with a history of suspicion of new males in their family life could co-exist with one middle-aged intellectual. Zack and Matt would fight, make each other laugh, punch each other hard and struggle over the dish of jellybeans in the office while, with variable effectiveness, Jenny would try to get them to behave themselves. I would try to listen to them and follow the thread of their conversation while at the same time honouring Jenny's concerns and the real problems that brought them to a counselling office rather than a video arcade. On occasions, I would set up a speaker's chair to give some order and ritual to our meetings. On other occasions I would have to plunge into a wrestling match over the jellybean dish; give Matt control over the video camera; stand up; invent games; or otherwise keep the session from dissolving into recess at a junior high school. I was not cool. I was no more nor less than a well intentioned guy trying to find a way to have conversation with two teenagers who were unsure about letting me in.

One evening, however, after months of my having been patient, non-directive and creative in *multi-directional partiality*, Zack continued to laugh and draw Matt into his usual role of jester while Jenny attempted to talk about serious worries she had about an incident at school involving Matt. I found myself furious. Even while the professional in me sought evenness and was concerned about appropriateness, something else in me had had it. Seeking to control the shaking in my voice, I confronted Zack with his incongruence.

> What are you doing? Huh? What are you doing? You say you want Matt to care more about his life and to stop being just a goof-off, but the minute Jenny talks about something she is concerned about you start this shit.

My anger was as much news to me as to the startled family. 'Chill out man,' said a chastened Zack. But I was not done with him.

'Doesn't all this matter to you? Why did you come today if you don't want to work on making things better?'

My own family can attest to the intrusive burden of my occasional judgemental outbursts, and in supervision I have had to work on my tendency to side with authority and to look for order. This was different. It was utterly unplanned, unstrategic, unwilled and unwelcome. It was not an attempt to get Zack to do something or to control Matt or to back up Mom. Though it was a furious reaction to Zack's behaviour, it was not judgemental in this way: I did not see myself as above Zack, correcting him with authority; I did not see myself as right or as the important voice in the room; I didn't have an intention to get some point across to Zack.

In this interview I asked the family about it. Jenny said:

> It had probably built up session after session . . . of just 'the Zack and Matt show'. We were not getting anywhere. I wondered why it took you so long to get mad. Sometimes with these two you have to hit them over the head with a hammer to even get their attention.

Zack said, 'It was embarrassing, but you had a perfectly good reason to be angry.' I asked what made him come back to later sessions: expression of counsellor judgement, however rationalized by clients, can mean the end of the counselling. He told me that if the anger had been unfair, he would maybe still have come back but not been all there.

Reflecting on the incident myself, I think if it had come much earlier in our sessions, the boys would not have come back. I would have been just another man trying to be the man of the house and using judgement and authority without having established caring, acceptance and commitment. In later sessions, I would perhaps have less reason for anger in that the boy's higher trust and greater maturity would have allowed for the kind of give-and-take that might preclude angry outbursts.

The counsellor experiences unconditional positive regard for the clients

I would usually meet alone with Jenny for at least part of every session. I did this partly to avoid long meetings with her and Matt, which would have the unintended but inevitable effect of having us get trapped into laying expectations on him. We also met so that Jenny could talk about what she was going through, was concerned about and was hoping for, without having to be in any way in role for her sons.

About those sessions Jenny said:

> You made me feel like I wasn't such a total loser mom. You did build me up in areas where I thought I was failing in the whole thing. You pointed out things that were obvious but that I couldn't see . . .
>
> One thing you said to the kids (when they were talking about what a loser their father was), 'You also have your mom's genes'. You said it to *them* but I heard it and took it in. They also have my genes. They can be strong. And do well.

When I asked what would *not* have been helpful in the counselling, she said:

> I think anybody who would judge you . . . why or how you do something. We are all in different situations and lord knows why or how we got there. [Counsellors] are there to help you get your way out of there, not to judge why you got in there!

In one of our sessions, I provided support and confirmation for her about her actions when she had overheard Zack talking on the telephone about a plan he had to use hallucinogenic drugs later that night at a park with friends. Embarrassed at having overheard the conversation (not a usual procedure in her household), she none-theless confronted Zack and told him that she did not want him taking those drugs. He argued back and challenged her to try and stop him. She neither lapsed into threats, nor backed away from her insistence that he not use the drugs. He stormed off and drove away in anger. Later that night, he returned and went to bed quietly. He had taken no drugs that night.

Feeling stuck, in the middle of counselling, between a desire to accept Matt as he was and frustration about how he was acting at school and home, I once wrote him a letter, read it aloud in a family meeting and gave each family member a copy (see Chapter 3 for a brief discussion of narrative therapy). I began by asking why we were continuing counselling and answered as follows:

> It is not because there is something wrong with you. You are sane, smart and likeable. You are OK and you have the equipment you need to live a good life. Is it because there is something wrong with your family life? No. You have love and intelligence from your mother and she is in there with you for the long haul. Is it to figure out how to relate to your father and how he has lived? I think we could talk about this more, but I know lots of people who have little to do with their fathers and have fathers

who have tough lives and still have a good life themselves. Is it to help you get along with and feel equal to your brother? Maybe, but you have not complained about this. It is clear that your brother loves and admires you (even while he is bossy with you and gives you a hard time). Most people survive brothers far less smart and good than yours. Is it because you and your family have troubles, fears, anger, frustrations and make mistakes? No, of course not – everybody has something that they have to battle against.

The reason I think we are meeting is because of a character we might call *Impulse*. *Impulse* is a guy who sometimes interferes in the lives of bright, likeable kids. He takes kids who are as smart, capable and promising as can be and tells them that they are not supposed to have a successful, peaceful life. *Impulse* tells kids that they can't be patient with boring or impolite teachers. He tells them that they cannot keep their mouths shut when a teacher is after them. *Impulse* tells kids to give up when work is hard or boring. He says don't bother about homework. He says, 'Don't take any crap from anybody – even if they are a school principal.' *Impulse* says, 'Don't talk with your mother or teachers about something you didn't do or don't want to do, just let things go and try to fake it. Maybe they will forget about what you do or don't do. Anyway don't worry today.' *Impulse* is really against your ever trying hard. *Impulse* would be really angry if you ever got an A or B in something besides choir or gym. *Impulse* wants you to get Fs and Ds. *Impulse* thinks that if you show people how smart you are, they will expect too much from you. *Impulse* says, 'Don't work hard. It's bad for you. It will make your brother jealous and your father sad.' *Impulse* says you are not supposed to have a life with any success except being funny and being liked.

When I wrote this letter, I was feeling a strong sense of losing psychological contact with all the individuals in this family. The letter was my response to this predicament: it was difficult to speak to Matt congruently without responding to the trouble that seemed to follow him every day. The letter was as much to his family and expressive of my feeling of their dilemma as it was to the young man. The invention of the character *Impulse* provided a temporary language which allowed affectionate appreciation of the boy without suppressing awareness of the behaviours which his family seemed to cut him off and isolate him in a career of avoidance. The mother of the family showed the letter to friends and said: 'I didn't know you could do that: separate the person from the behaviour that way.'

About the counselling, Zack said:

I like the fact that you didn't really criticize anything . . . You don't say what's right or wrong. I think it would be bad if somebody said: 'Oh, no, no . . . You need to do things *this* way in order to be happy . . .'

In fact, I had and have many opinions about right and wrong, some of which I expressed; others, fortunately, I put aside in service of my first intention, which was to connect with all three people in this family. I was concerned about Jenny not being pushed around – for the boys' sake as well as hers. The boys sometimes played rough tricks on their smaller mother that made it seem more like she was someone who belonged to them rather than a person deserving of respect. I challenged their right to continue with horseplay with her after she had told them to stop. Sometimes I would say: 'Jenny, did you just ask Matt to stop doing that?' Sometimes: 'Hey! Cut it out!'

I wanted to help get Matt out of the role of easy target for his teachers' negative focus. A pattern was developing in which Matt, with friends his highest priority and struggling with impulse, would keep getting in trouble for talking when talking was not allowed. In a vestige of the educational system I was in decades earlier, the teachers would feel free to talk to him in a rough and angry way. Matt, maintaining his adolescent dignity and not raised with the assumption (as I was) that 'of course adults would oppress you', would talk back and then be sent by an indignant teacher to the vice principal to be suspended, threatened with expulsion or otherwise punished. I would role play the teachers' furious voices: 'I'm a teacher. Something must be wrong with me. I can't even get these little 13-year-olds to cooperate. Well I'll show them! If this kid says anything insulting to me, I will really get him!' Matt's trips to the vice principal's office and suspensions decreased.

I became aware of how, as a youthful-looking single parent, Jenny sometimes seemed to be patronized by Matt's school authorities and, on one occasion, was even treated as though she were covering up for Matt. I was indignant on her behalf and encouraged confrontation of their implicit disrespect and condescension. Similarly, when it seemed that Matt's punishments at school were out of proportion to his offences, I actively joined with her in considering whether and how she should intervene.

In general, I supported Jenny's decision-making about consequences for Matt's avoiding school assignments and, when asked, about Zack's explosive expression of anger. A lot of times I persisted in asking Matt to put words to what he felt rather than just joking. As expressed above, I took it upon myself to ask questions about Rick rather than take for granted a one-dimensional picture of the boys' father.

I believe that a relational counsellor must face the paradox of being a thinking person and a resource about family living as well as a facilitator for family members' own decision-making about 'what's right and wrong'.

The counsellor experiences *empathy* for the clients' internal frame of reference

In some sessions, at my request, Matt brought in his skateboard. We went outside for him to educate me in skateboarding in general as well as for him to show me his way of doing it and the tricks he would be using in a contest coming up. How could a 12-year-old talk except while he was occupied in a way natural to him?

On one occasion I invited Matt to bring in a much criticized school bag he had, in which was contained 'lost' homework, old books, a magazine about skateboarding, collections of odds and ends, ancient incomplete assignments and teachers' notes. I let him know that the school bag reminded me of my own school days in which keeping track of things and keeping things in any sort of order had seemed beyond me. I told him about an incident when I was in the seventh grade (his year). My teacher had come down to my desk and thrown everything in it out onto the floor in the unrealized hope that embarrassment would make me neater. (We were linked by a system that acted as if shame was the way to bring about order and discipline!) After several weeks he did bring in his school bag. The two of us went through it, discussing every item – its purpose and his feelings about it. I was able to learn what was important, frustrating, useful and fun. Most important, perhaps, was that Matt showed the school bag to someone who was interested in it, but did not judge it. I was interested in what was interesting to him.

It is important to note that, as in all counselling, the counsellor is connecting with the client about events, items and meanings that are important to the client. With a less verbal client like Matt, it was important to connect about school bags and skateboards. On one occasion because one family meeting was taken up by Matt's attempts to talk his mother into buying him expensive tickets to see a rock group notorious for angry, obscene lyrics and a large following of adolescent males, I asked Matt to make a tape of the group. Through his effort, I got to hear music and lyrics, typical of which was the phrase 'I ain't got enough middle fingers'. This was not a patronizing attempt to appear cool, but a way to hear some of what in the world was important to him.

Zack knew how to get the most out of family sessions. He was able to put out his immediate distress and gain the attention and concern of both the counsellor, Matt and his mother. Matt also would feel freer to share more when the subject was Zack rather than himself. In our last session, Matt was articulate on the subject of fairness for everyone concerned, as the family talked about adjustment to the increasing presence of Zack's girlfriend. About the effects of the family listening-in session to his lengthy and vigorous expression of anger, Zack said:

> I like letting off steam like that. I like having people listen to me. It takes a patient person to do that, I know. It calms me down if somebody will sit there and just take in what I have to say – I mean like what I'm mad *about*. If I'm all mad and somebody says: 'Oh just shut up. You're just having a temper tantrum,' it makes me even madder. I'll just dig myself into a hole. I'll get so mad I don't know what I'm doing.

About individual counselling he had experienced at the age of about six, Zack said:

> It was cool just to have somebody to listen to my problems. He would try to help me with things that pissed me off instead of just accusing me of being a bad kid. It was nice to have an older friend that would listen to me and try to help me without labelling me a problem child.

Clients are at least to a minimum degree able to perceive these qualities

In our review interview, Matt indicated that he would like the sessions to continue – not very often, but sometimes. A counsellor would be 'someone to talk to. We could have meetings with my mom and me and sometimes meetings with Zack and mom and me.' I made a deal to continue.

How could Matt see that I was aware of him as equally complex and interesting when in the presence of his articulate, goal-oriented brother? How could he be neither left to fade into the background of the conversation nor brought under the spotlight in a way which embarrassed or trapped him? How could I listen respectfully and carefully to the talkative Zack while at the same time making room in the conversation for his mother and brother? How could I be on Jenny's side as a mother deserving respect without turning into another male trying to take illegitimate authority in a family to which he did not belong?

In relational counselling, it takes one person who is committed to the process to get things started. Little counselling would have been possible if Jenny had not persisted in asking the boys to come in the face of the awkwardness and inconvenience of difficult conversations. After that, my job was to be there for all family members, not only demonstrating respect for their individual interests, but also adapting to their differing styles and developmental tasks. Alone, after sessions, and sometimes in supervision, I reflected on how I connected with each family member and how respectful I was of that person's point of view. Sometimes in the next session, I would take up an issue or a statement that had seemed overlooked in the intensity of the moment. I frequently would ask for individual check-in time with each member to find out how counselling seemed to them. Multi-directional partiality does not require agreeing with all family members all the time. The process does ask for commitment to be aware of each member's reaction to the counselling conversation.

The formative directional tendency

My wife Martha's comment on my passenger seat driving, 'How do you think I get *anywhere* safely when you are not with me?' is useful for reflection on work with families (although it has not significantly changed my behaviour when being driven by her). I am helpful to families only if I assume I am working with already existing tendencies toward greater order, greater individuality and greater cooperation among themselves. Carl Rogers threw out a challenge for counsellors:

> Thus when we provide a psychological climate that permits persons to *be*
> – whether they are clients, students, workers, or persons in a group – we
> are not involved in a chance event. We are tapping into a tendency which
> permeates all of organic life – a tendency to become all the complexity of
> which the organism is capable. (1980: 134)

Once when preparing tapes of the Clark family for a presentation in Scotland, I worked with a local video technician who said, *unasked* and echoing the thoughts of at least one man with whom Jeremy had been involved: 'Those boys need a father. They are running wild. They need someone to control them'. If I had attempted to be a temporary authoritarian father, as he implied was needed, or if I had formulated a treatment plan for them that included teaching Jenny an outsider's approach to discipline, I would not have been a helpful counsellor. In fact, Jenny had her own concerns about her ability to expect limits and self-control from the boys. We *reframed* (see Chapter 3) by describing her as a mother who was now getting to the second of two tasks: the first was to be there for her boys with unlimited love and attention; the second, and now more timely, was to ask of her boys the same respect for others and responsibility for their lives that she holds as her own highest values. Trusting the ability of the family to sort out the interaction of accountability and love was a matter of discussion, mistakes and affirming moments such as Jenny and Zack's confrontation over drugs.

Asked what characterized the family, Zack said:

> We are pretty open, I have to say, but not always in a good way. We pretty much share everything with each other as far as feelings go . . . such openness, you know, kind of helps if you need to talk about something, you know?

Asked what made the family be so open, he said: 'My mom.' She agreed: 'He's right. I'm always . . . "we have to talk about it . . . family meeting!"' I asked when they started having family meetings and she replied: 'From the beginning. When they were real little.'

Jenny said, 'We are all close in different ways. Even Zack and Matt are really close to each other.' Zack and she disagreed the most, she reflected, but they always communicated. Matt and she talked less together but were always comfortable just hanging out together. Her oldest son (who, I swear, has never heard the name Carl Rogers) said about her: *'Probably the main thing she gives us is unconditional love.'*

A major theme of the counselling was how the two boys could live in the same household and share the same room. How, in particular, could the family deal with Zack's self-centredness and anger and urge to have things his way? How could the family deal with Matt's lack of direct expression of feelings; his lack of expression of goals; his inclination to joke in the face of challenge?

The following exchange took place near the end of the review interview. We were talking about Zack's anger and what it took for him to express it and let go of it. I asked Matt if he got angry. He joked 'What you ask me that question for, huh, punk?' – a typical response for him. His mother said, 'You do get angry. You got angry at Zack the other day.' 'Oh yeah,' said his older brother and continued:

> *Zack*: I wrote him this big long note – that was cool how he handled that. Because normally, you know, I scream and yell at Matt. And he screams and yells back and nothing really comes of it. All we did [this time] is . . . we wrote notes to each other.
> The last time he really made me mad about a situation we normally yell about, I just figured I needed to write a letter about how I feel so he wouldn't say anything back or whatever? [laughs] So I stuck the note on the door and he picked it up and then he wrote a letter back to me – so I could kind of take, you know, the way he felt about stuff too. It was really much more effective that he really wrote a letter to me. That was pretty cool, Matt, I have to say. I was kind of expecting to come back and find my room all messed up.
> *Matt*: I was about to throw [something] right across the room, but I was like . . . 'Wait . . .'
> *Zack*: That was way cool – that you wrote that letter.

I told their mother that she looked proud, but she was reflecting back on Matt's anger and talked about how mad he had been and that she had thought he had been going to trash Zack's room. Matt answered her with intensity – the most directly, confronting, non-joking I ever saw him – 'I didn't say that. I didn't *even* say that.'

I tried to track the conversation. Was Jenny saying that it was her idea that Matt would answer Zack's letter with another letter? No, she had not made that suggestion. She had simply listened to some of Matt's first angry reaction. I asked him: 'When did you know that you would write a letter back to your brother, Matt?' 'The minute I read it', he replied.

The boys had handled something on their own. The two sons whose father was out there, living in his car or in motels, had written each other respectful notes about their dispute about how to use the room with friends and how to leave the other's things alone. Their mother, who had worried about how she was doing with them, was not needed as they worked something out. In addition, for the first time in the counselling, two things had happened: firstly, Zack, unprompted, had gone out of his way to positively acknowledge his younger brother; and secondly, Matt had directly expressed person-to-person disagreement without turning it into a joke. He had had the self-esteem to put forward and defend his own version of a story. Could the video technician or various candidates for the job of stepfather have done a better job with this family than they were learning to do themselves?

Afterword

There is more *doorknob* counselling when working with families and couples than with individuals. There are more people to talk to on the way out the door; more reassurances sought, opinions asked and sometimes, I'm afraid, opinions given. So it is with this book. What is left out? Lots. I have been thinking and learning about relational counselling for more than 20 years. I have not addressed the question of training specifically for family and couples counselling and, except in passing, the book has not discussed approaches to family of origin or ways to use adult knowledge, strength and skills to renew and revise connections with parents and siblings.

Here at the doorknob, there is not time for lengthy discussion of training. Relational counselling is an art form that requires efforts, intentions and cultivation additional to one's preparation for individual work. My own training included classes, workshops and immersion in books and articles about family and couples counselling on its own terms. Most importantly, I found supervisors who respected me and had a philosophy compatible with the person-centred approach who had spent thousands of hours in the world of couples and families. I observed their work, did co-therapy, and was observed on video, audio and behind a one-way mirror. Mostly I talked with them in the oldest style of supervision, letting conversation sort out what were *my* problems, strengths, needs and hopes and what belonged to my clients.

Interest in the exploration of family of origin emerges in any lengthy contact with clients or counsellors in training. The process of individual counselling often naturally includes exploration and revision of the self-concept in relation to the significant others of one's childhood experience. A rich literature exists (for example, Framo, 1992; Boszormenyi-Nagy and Krassner, 1986; Bowen, 1978) which may add an objective dimension to clients' and counsellors' searches to revise their early, so influential relationships. As simple an exercise as a genogram or personalised family map (McGoldrick and Gerson, 1985) can extend empathy into the subjective situation of persons formerly seen only in stagnant memories shaped by childhood powerlessness.

How has 20 years' experience with families and couples made me feel more helpful than when I began seeing more than one person at once?

My 20 years have given me consistent feedback that clients always *react negatively to perceived counsellor judgement.* They will usually catch us if we try to be clever or manipulative; will most of the time react positively to perceived counsellor empathy; and will almost always seek to find out about the persons we genuinely are. To be frank, I have found myself judging more times than I can count and neglecting empathy in favour of some lesson I thought I urgently needed to teach.

I have learned to notice and work with the client who is most likely to be or to feel judged. This feeling of being evaluated negatively is the most common experience in the painful side of relational living (see Rogers, 1961b: 330, for his realization of this persistent factor in breakdowns in communication). If I gently contact the person feeling most judged I can bring her into congruent participation and reduce the mistrust and distance of others present.

I have learned to expect that clients will allow me to facilitate. Clients have an investment in allowing counsellors to allow them to talk together. With rare exceptions, they will do so, *if* they feel that they will also have a turn to be heard.

I try to remember that the clients' ideas will hold the key to successful change. Twenty years have given me less cause to expect that my great insights will make a difference and much cause to expect that, if I am listening for it, some unfancy client remark will provide the key to the family or couple's next step. I am convinced that the relational counsellor is like a good teacher who is eagerly looking for subtle changes in her learners' perceptions of their situation.

I have also learned to be active and verbal with clients while living out the core conditions of the person-centred approach in the intensity of the counselling sessions. Activity is essential when working with more than one individual, and can be consistent with the person-centred approach if one maintains multi-directional partiality.

The principles of the person-centred approach have become the deepest foundation for my work with any number of people in complex situations.

> We shall not cease from exploration
> And the end of all our exploring
> Will be to arrive where we started
> And know the place for the first time
> T.S. Eliot

The best relational counsellor occupies the somewhat paradoxical position of the *confident beginner*, of which Carl Rogers was the master. The greatest gift he consistently offered was his willingness to learn from and with his clients.

References

American Association of Marriage and Family Therapists (1995) *Special Issue: The Effectiveness of Marital and Family Therapy, Journal of Marital and Family Therapy*, 21 (4).

Anderson, H. (1997) *Conversation, Language and Possibilities: A Postmodern Approach to Therapy*. New York: Basic Books.

Anderson, W.J. (1989a) 'Family therapy in the client-centered tradition: a legacy in the narrative mode', *Person Centered Review*, 4 (3): 295–307.

Anderson, W.J. (1989b) 'Client-centered approaches to couple and family therapy: expanding theory and practice', *Person Centered Review*, 4 (3): 425–7.

Anonymous (1972) 'Toward the differentiation of self in one's own family', in J.L. Framo (ed.), *Family Interaction*. New York: Springer.

Aponte, H.J. (1976) 'The family school interview', *Family Process*, 15: 303–10.

Aponte, H.J. (1994) 'How personal can training get?' *Journal of Marital and Family Therapy*, 20 (1): 3–15.

Barrett, B. (1996) 'An Insider's View of Marriage', *Living Better*, San Diego, CA.

Barrett-Lennard, G.T. (1984) 'The world of family relationships: a person-centered systems view', in R.F. Levant and J.M. Shlien (eds), *Client-Centered Therapy and the Person-Centered Approach*. New York: Praeger. pp. 222–42.

Barrett-Lennard, G.T. (1998) *Carl Rogers' Helping System: Journey and Substance*. London: Sage.

Bateson, G. (1979) *Mind and Nature*. New York: Dutton.

Bateson, G., Jackson, D.D., Haley, J. and Weakland, J.H. (1956) 'Toward a theory of schizophrenia', *Behavioral Science*, 1: 251–64.

Berg, I.K. and Miller, S.D. (1992) *Working With the Problem Drinker: A Solution-Focused Approach*. New York: Norton.

Boszormenyi-Nagy, I. and Krassner, B. (1986) *Between Give and Take: A Clinical Guide to Contextual Therapy*. New York: Brunner/Mazel.

Boszormenyi-Nagy, I. and Ulrich, D. (1981) 'Contextual family therapy', in A.S. Gurman and D.P. Kniskern (eds), *Handbook of Family Therapy*. New York: Brunner/Mazel. pp. 159–86.

Boszormenyi-Nagy, I., Grunebaum, J. and Ulrich, D. (1991) 'Contextual therapy', in A.S. Gurman and D.P. Kniskern (eds), *Handbook of Family Therapy, Volume 2*. New York: Brunner/Mazel. pp. 200–39.

Bowen, M. (1978) *Family Therapy in Clinical Practice*. New York: Jason Aronson.

Bozarth, J.D. (1984) 'Beyond reflection: emergent modes of empathy', in R.F. Levant and J.M. Schlien (eds), *Client-Centered Therapy and the Person-Centered Approach*. New York: Praeger. pp. 222–42.

Bozarth, J.D. and Shanks, A. (1989) 'Person-centered family therapy with couples', *Person Centered Review*, 4 (3): 280–94.

Bray, J.H. and Jouriles, E.N. (1995) 'Treatment of marital conflict and prevention of divorce', *Journal of Marital and Family Therapy*, 21 (4): 461–73.

Broderick, C.B. and Schrader, S.S. (1991) 'The history of professional marriage and family therapy', in A.S. Gurman and D.P. Kniskern (eds), *Handbook of Family Therapy, Volume 2*. New York: Brunner/Mazel. pp. 3–41.

Brown, L.S. and Zimmer, D. (1986) 'An introduction to therapy issues of lesbian and gay male couples', in N.J. Jacobson and A.S. Gurman (eds), *Clinical Handbook of Marital Therapy*. New York: Guilford. pp. 451–71.

Cain, D.J. (1989) 'From the individual to the family', *Person Centered Review*, 4 (3): 248–55.

Carl, D. (1990) *Counseling Same-Sex Couples*. New York: Norton.

Carter, B. (1986) 'Success in family therapy', *The Family Therapy Networker*, 10 (4): 17–22.

Carter, B. (1989) 'Gender sensitive therapy', *The Family Therapy Networker*, 13 (4): 57–62.

Carter, B. (1992) 'Stonewalling feminism', *The Family Therapy Networker*, 16 (1): 60–4.

Cechin, G., Lane, G. and Ray, W.A. (1993) 'From strategizing to nonintervention: toward irreverence in systemic practice', *Journal of Marital and Family Therapy*, 19 (2): 125–36.

Chambers, N. (1998) Personal communication.

Clark, W.M. and Serovich, J.M. (1997) 'Twenty years and still in the dark? Content analysis of articles pertaining to gay, lesbian and bi-sexual issues in marriage and family journals', *Journal of Marital and Family Therapy*, 23 (3): 239–53.

Combs, A.W. (1989) *A Theory of Therapy*. Newbury Park, CA: Sage.

Cordova, J., Jacobson, N. and Christensen, A. (1977) 'Acceptance versus change interventions in behavioural couple therapy: impact on couples' in-session communication', *Journal of Marital and Family Therapy*, 24 (4): 437–55.

Duncan, B.L. (1992) 'Strategic therapy, eclecticism and the therapeutic relationship', *Journal of Marital and Family Therapy*, 18 (1): 24–30.

Duncan, B.L., Hubble, M.A. and Miller, S.D. (1997a) 'Stepping off the throne', *The Family Therapy Networker*, 21 (4): 22–33.

Duncan, B.L., Hubble, M.A. and Miller, S.D. (1997b) *Escape from Babel: Toward a Unifying Language for Psychotherapy Practice*. New York: Norton.

Duncan, B.L., Hubble, M.A. and Miller, S.D. (1997c) *Psychotherapy with 'Impossible' Cases*. New York: Norton.

Efran, J., Greene, M. and Gordon, D. (1998) 'Lessons of the new genetics', *The Family Therapy Networker*, 22 (2): 26–30; 35–40.

Ellinwood, C. (1989) 'The young child in person-centred family therapy', *Person-Centred Review*, 4 (3): 256–61.

Epston, D. (1994) 'Extending the conversation: letters can be power tools for reauthoring lives', *The Family Therapy Networker*, 18 (6): 30–7, 62–3.

Falicov, C.J. (1986) 'Cross-cultural marriages', in N.J. Jacobson and A.S. Gurman (eds), *Clinical Handbook of Marital Therapy*. New York: Guilford. pp. 429–51.

Falicov, C.J. (1998) 'Commentary on Hoffman: from rigid borderline to fertile borderlands: reconfiguring family therapy', *Journal of Marital and Family Therapy*, 24 (2): 157–65.

Farson, R. (1996) *Management of the Absurd*. New York: Simon and Schuster.

Farson, R. (1987) 'Dick Farson with the community', *Living Now Institute*: Center For Studies of the Person. La Jolla, CA.

Fisch, R., Weakland, J.H. and Segal, L. (1982) *The Tactics of Change: Doing Therapy Briefly*. New York: Jossey-Bass.

Framo, J.L. (1981) 'The integration of marital therapy with sessions with family of origin', in A.S. Gurman and D.P. Kniskern (eds), *Handbook of Family Therapy, Volume 1*. New York: Brunner/Mazel. pp. 133–58.

Framo, J.L. (1992) *Family of Origin Therapy: An Intergenerational Approach*. New York: Brunner/Mazel.

Framo, J.L. (1996) 'A personal retrospective of the family therapy field: then and now', *Journal of Marital and Family Therapy*, 22 (3): 289–316.

Freedman, J. and Combs, G. (1996) *Narrative Therapy: The Social Construction of Preferred Realities*. New York: Norton.

Friedman, E. (1991) 'Bowen theory and therapy', in A.S. Gurman and D.P. Kniskern (eds), *Handbook of Family Therapy, Volume 2*. New York: Brunner/Mazel. pp. 134–71.

Gaylin, N.L. (1989) 'The necessary and sufficient conditions for change: individual versus family therapy', *Person Centered Review*, 4 (3): 263–79.

Gaylin, N.L. (1990) 'Roundtable discussion', *Person Centered Review*, 5 (4): 470–72.

Gaylin, N.L. (1993) 'Person centred family therapy', in D. Brazier (ed.), *Beyond Carl Rogers*. London: Constable. pp. 181–201.

Gendlin, E.T. (1970) 'A theory of personality change', in J.T. Hart and T.M. Tomlinson (eds), *New Directions in Client-Centered Therapy*. Boston: Houghton Mifflin. pp. 129–73.

Gendlin, E.T. (1984) 'The client's client: the edge of awareness', in R.F. Levant and J.M. Schlien (eds), *Client-Centered Therapy and the Person Centered Approach*. New York: Praeger.

Goolishian, H.A. and Anderson H. (1992) 'Strategy and intervention versus nonintervention: a matter of theory', *Journal of Marital and Family Therapy*, 18 (1): 5–15.

Gordon, T. (1975) *P.E.T. Parent Effectiveness Training*. New York: Plume Books.

Gordon, T. (1988) 'The case against disciplining children at home or in school', *Person Centered Review*, 3 (1): 59–86.

Gottman, J.M. (1991) 'Predicting the longitudinal course of marriages', *Journal of Marital and Family Therapy*, 17 (1): 3–7.

Gottman, J.M. (1994) 'An agenda for marital therapy', in S.M. Johnson and L.S. Greenberg (eds), *The Heart of the Matter: Perspectives on Emotion in Marital Therapy*. New York: Brunner/Mazel. pp. 256–97.

Gottman, J.M. (1994) *Why Marriages Succeed and Fail . . . and How You Can Make Yours Last*. New York: Simon and Schuster.

Gottman, J.M., Notarius, C., Gonso, J. and Markman, H. (1976) *A Couple's Guide to Communication*. Champaign, IL: Research.

Greenberg, L.S. and Johnson, S.M. (1986) 'Emotionally focused therapy for couples', in N.J. Jacobson and A.S. Gurman (eds), *Clinical Handbook of Marital Therapy*. New York: Guilford. pp. 253–79.

Guerney, B.G. (1984) 'Contributions of client-centered therapy to filial, marital and family relationship enhancement therapies', in R.F. Levant and J.M. Schlien (eds), *Client-Centered Therapy and the Person-Centered Approach*. New York: Praeger. pp. 261–77.

Guerney, B.G. (1994) 'The role of emotion in relationship enhancement marital/family therapy', in S.M. Johnson and L.S. Greenberg (eds), *The Heart of the Matter: Perspectives on Emotion in Marital Therapy*. New York: Brunner/Mazel. pp. 124–51.

Guerney, B.G. (1998) 'Revitalizing intimacy', *Twenty-First Family Therapy Network Symposium*, Relationship Enhancement Day Workshop. Washington, D.C.

Guerney, B.G. and Mason, P. (1990) 'Marital and family enrichment research: a decade review and look ahead', *Journal of Marriage and the Family*, 52: 1127–35.

Gurman, A.S. and Kniskern, D.P. (eds) (1981) *Handbook of Family Therapy, Volume 1*. New York: Brunner/Mazel.

Gurman, A.S. and Kniskern, D.P. (eds) (1991) *Handbook of Family Therapy, Volume 2*. New York: Brunner/Mazel.

Guttman, H.A. (1991) 'Systems theory, cybernetics and epistomology', in A.S. Gurman and D.P. Kniskern (eds), *Handbook of Family Therapy, Volume 2*. New York: Brunner/Mazel. pp. 41–65.

Haley, J. (1963) *Strategies of Psychotherapy*. New York: Grune and Stratton.

Haley, J. (1973) *Uncommon Therapy*. New York: Norton.

Haley, J. (1976) *Problem-Solving Therapy: New Strategies for Effective Family Therapy*. San Francisco: Jossey-Bass.

Haley, J. (1980) *Leaving Home*. New York: McGraw-Hill.

Haley, J. (1982) *Reflection on Therapy and Other Issues*. Chevy Chase, MD: Family Therapy Institute of Washington, D.C.

Hart, J.T. and Tomlinson, T.M. (eds) (1970) *New Directions in Client-Centered Therapy*. Boston: Houghton Mifflin.

Hoffman, L. (1990) 'Constructing realities: an art of lenses', *Family Process*, 29 (1): 1–12.

Hoffman, L. (1998) 'Setting aside the model in family therapy', *Journal of Marital and Family Therapy*, 24 (2): 145–57.

Imber-Black, E. (1991) 'A family – larger systems perspective', in A.S. Gurman and D.P. Kniskern (eds), *Handbook of Family Therapy, Volume 2*. New York: Brunner/Mazel. pp. 583–606.

Johnson, S.M. (1997) 'The biology of love: what therapists need to know about attachment', *The Family Therapy Networker*, 21 (5): 36–41.

Johnson, S.M. (1998) 'Creating healing relations for couples dealing with trauma: the use of emotionally focused marital therapy', *Journal of Marital and Family Therapy*, 24 (1): 3–24.

Johnson, S.M. and Greenberg, L.S. (1994a) 'Emotion in intimate relationships: a synthesis', in *The Heart of the Matter: Perspectives on Emotion in Marital Therapy*. New York: Brunner/Mazel. pp. 297–325.

Johnson, S.M. and Greenberg, L.S. (eds) (1994b) *The Heart of the Matter: Perspectives on Emotion in Marital Therapy*. New York: Brunner/Mazel.

Kirschenbaum, H. (1979) *On Becoming Carl Rogers*. New York: Delacorte Press.

Kirschenbaum, H. and Henderson, V. (eds) (1990) *Carl Rogers: Dialogues*. London: Constable.

Kirschenbaum, H. and Henderson, V. (eds) (1990) *The Carl Rogers Reader*. London: Constable.

Kleckner, T., Frank, L., Bland, C., Amendt, J.H. and Bryant, R.D. (1992) 'The myth of the unfeeling strategic therapist', *Journal of Marital and Family Therapy*, 18 (1): 41–51.

Knudson-Martin, C. (1997) 'The politics of gender in family therapy', *Journal of Marital and Family Therapy*, 23 (4): 421–39.

Koerner, K. and Jacobson, N.S. (1994) 'Emotion and behavioral couple therapy', in *The Heart of the Matter: Perspectives on Emotion in Marital Therapy*. New York: Brunner/Mazel. pp. 2207–27.

Layton, M. (1995) 'Mastering mindfulness', *The Family Therapy Networker*, 19 (6): 28–30, 57.

Lebow, J. (1997) 'Is couples therapy obsolete? Psychoeducation raises questions about traditional clinical approaches', *The Family Therapy Networker*, 21 (5): 81–8.

Levant, R.F. (1984) 'From person to system: two perspectives', in R.F. Levant and J.M. Shlien (eds), *Client-Centered Therapy and the Person-Centered Approach*. New York: Praeger. pp. 261–77.

Levant, R.F. (1997) 'Commentary on Knudson-Martin gender equality and the new psychology of man', *Journal of Marital and Family Therapy*, 23 (4): 439–45.

Levant, R.F. and Schlien J.M. (eds) (1984) *Client-Centered Therapy and the Person-Centered Approach*. New York: Praeger.

Mace, D.R. and Mace V. (1986) 'Marriage enrichment – developing interpersonal potential', in P. Dial and R. Jewson (eds.), *In Praise of Fifty Years: The Groves Conference on the Conservation of Marriage and the Family*. Lake Mills, IA: Graphic.

Madanes, C. (1981) *Strategic Family Therapy*. San Francisco: Jossey-Bass.

Madigan, S. (1994) 'The discourse unnoticed: story-telling rights and the deconstruction of longstanding problems', *Journal of Child and Youth Care*, 9 (2): 79–86.

Markowitz, L.M. (1994) 'When same sex couples divorce', *The Family Therapy Networker*, 18 (3): 30–31.

McGoldrick, M. and Gerson, R. (1985) *Genograms in Family Assessment*. New York: Norton.

McGoldrick, M., Pierce, J.K. and Giordano, J. (eds) (1982) *Ethnicity and Family Therapy*. New York: Guilford.

Mearns, D. (1991) 'The unspoken relationship between psychotherapist and client', paper presented at the Second International Conference on Client-centered and Experiential Psychotherapy, Stirling, Scotland.

Mearns, D. (1994a) *Developing Person Centred Counselling*. London: Sage.

Mearns, D. (1994b) 'How to work with a couple?', in *Developing Person Centred Counselling*. London: Sage. pp. 56–60.

Mearns, D. (1995) 'Supervision: a tale of the missing client', *British Journal of Guidance and Counselling*, 23 (3): 421–27.

Mearns, D. (1997) *Person-Centred Counselling Training*. London: Sage.

Mearns, D. (1999) 'Person-centred therapy with configuration of self', *Counselling*, 10 (2): 1–6.

Mearns, D. and Dryden, W. (eds) (1989) *Experiences of Counselling in Action*. London: Sage.

Mearns, D. and Thorne, B. (1988) *Person-Centred Counselling in Action*. London: Sage.

Miller, S.D., Hubble, M. and Duncan, B. (1995) 'No more bells and whistles', *The Family Therapy Networker*, 19 (2): 53–63.

Minuchin, S. (1974) *Families and Family Therapy*. Cambridge, MA: Harvard University Press.

Minuchin, S. and Nichols, M.P. (1993) *Family Healing: Tales of Hope and Renewal from Family Therapy*. New York: The Free Press.

Neill, J.R. and Kniskern, D.P. (1982) *From Psyche to System: The Evolving Therapy of Carl Whitaker*. New York: Guilford.

O'Hanlon, W. (1994) 'The third wave: can a brief therapy open doors to transformation?' *The Family Therapy Networker*, 18 (6): 18–29.

O'Hanlon, W.H. and Wiener-Davis, M. (1989) *In Search of Solutions*. New York: Norton.

O'Hara, M. (1996) 'Divided we stand', *The Family Therapy Networker*, 20 (5): 46–54.

O'Leary, C.J. (1989) 'The person-centered approach and family therapy: a dialogue between two traditions', *Person Centered Review*, 4 (3): 308–23.

Ono, L.M.L., de Haes, J.C.J.M., Hoos, A.M. and Lammes, F.B. (1995) 'Doctor-patient communication: a review of the literature', *Social Science Medicine*, 40 (7): 904–18.

Papp, P. (1983) *The Process of Change*. New York: Guilford.

Papp, P. (1984) 'The creative leap: the links between clinical and artistic creativity', *The Family Therapy Networker*, 8 (5): 20–29.

Papp, P. (1996) 'Listening to the system', *The Family Therapy Networker*, 21 (1): 52–58.

Papp, P. (1998) Personal communication.

Perske, R. and Perske, M. (1988) *Circles of Friends: People with Disabilities and their Friends Enrich the Lives of One Another*. Nashville, TN: Abingdon Press.

Prather, H. and Prather, G. (1988) *A Book for Couples*. New York: Doubleday.

Raskin, N.J. and Van der Veen, F. (1970) 'Client-centered family therapy: some clinical and research perspectives', in J.T. Hart and T.M. Tomlimson (eds), *New Directions in Client-Centered Therapy*. New York: Houghton-Mifflin. pp. 387–406.

Rogers, C.R. (1951) *Client Centred Therapy*. Boston: Houghton Mifflin.

Rogers, C.R. (1957) 'The necessary and sufficient conditions of therapeutic personality change', *Journal of Counseling Psychology*, 21 (2): 95–103.

Rogers, C.R. (1959) 'A theory of therapy, personality and interpersonal relationships as developed in the client-centered framework', in S. Koch (ed.), *Psychology: a Study of a Science. Volume 3. Formulations of the Person and the Social Contract*. New York: McGraw-Hill. pp. 184–256.

Rogers, C.R. (1961a) 'A tentative formulation of a general law of inter-personal relationships', in *On Becoming a Person*. Boston: Houghton Mifflin. pp. 338–47.

Rogers, C.R. (1961b) 'Dealing with breakdowns in communication – interpersonal and intergroup', in *On Becoming a Person*. Boston: Houghton Mifflin. pp. 329–38.

Rogers, C.R. (1961c) 'The implications of client-centered therapy for family life', in *On Becoming a Person*. Boston: Houghton Mifflin. pp. 314–29.

Rogers, C.R. (1961d) *On Becoming a Person*. Boston: Houghton Mifflin.

Rogers, C.R. (1967) 'Autobiography', in E.W. Boring and G. Lindzey (eds), *A History of Psychology in Autobiography, Vol. V*. New York: Appleton-Century-Crofts. pp. 343–84.

Rogers, C.R. (1972a) *Becoming Partners: Marriage and its Alternatives*. New York: Delta.

Rogers, C.R. (1972b) *Person To Person: Parent and Adolescent*. Unpublished. La Jolla CA: Center for Studies of the Person, Carl Rogers Research Center.

Rogers, C.R. (1978) 'The formative tendency', *Journal of Humanistic Psychology*, 18 (1): 23–26.

Rogers, C.R. (1979) Counselling Demonstration, Living Now Institute, Center for Studies of the Person, La Jolla, CA.

Rogers, C.R. (1980) *A Way of Being*. Boston: Houghton Mifflin.

Rogers, C.R. and Buber, M. (1990) 'Martin Buber', in H. Kirschenbaum and V. Henderson (eds), *Carl Rogers: Dialogues*. London: Constable. pp. 41–64.

Rowan, J. (1990) *Subpersonalities*. London: Routledge.

Sanders, D. (1997) Personal communication.

Satir, V. (1964) *Conjoint Family Therapy*. Palo Alto, CA: Science and Behavior Books.

Satir, V. (1972) *Perceptions: the Personal Aspects of Therapy*. Videotape: The Boston Family Institute.

Schwarz, R. (1987) 'Our multiple selves', *The Family Therapy Networker*, 11 (2): 24–31, 80–85.

Seligman, M.E.P. (1990) *Learned Optimism*. New York: Pocket Books.

de Shazer, S. (1985) *Keys to Solutions in Brief Therapy*. New York: Norton.

Shein, E.H. (1987) *Process Consultation, Vol. 2*. Reading, MA: Addison-Wesley.

Simon, R. (1984) 'Stranger in a strange land: an interview with Salvador Minuchin', *The Family Therapy Networker*, 8 (6): 20–32.

Simon, R. (1985) 'The take it or leave it therapy of Carl Whitaker', *The Family Therapy Networker*, 9 (5): 26–42.

Simon, R. (1997) 'Fearless foursome: an interview with the women's project', *The Family Therapy Networker*, 21 (6): 58–68.

Skynner, A.C.R. (1976) *Systems of Family and Marital Psychotherapy*. New York: Brunner/Mazel.

Snyder, M. (1989) 'The relationship enhancement model of couple therapy: an integration of Rogers and Bateson', *Person Centered Review*, 4 (3): 358–384.

Stanton, M.D. and Todd, T.C. (1982) *The Family Therapy of Drug Abuse and Addiction*. New York: Guilford.

Stuart, R.B. (1980) *Helping Couples Change: A Social Learning Approach to Marital Therapy*. New York: Guilford.

Stuart, R.B. (1989) 'Cognitive-behavioural couple therapy', Workshop at California Association of Marriage and Family Therapists' Annual Conference. San Diego, CA.

Stuart, R.B. and Jacobson, B. (1987) *Couple's Therapy Workbook*. Champaign, IL: Research Press.

Suchman, A.L., Roter, D., Green, M., Lipkin, M. and The Collaborative Study Group of the American Academy on Physician and Patient (1993) 'Physician satisfaction with primary care office visits', *Medical Care*, 31 (12): 1083–92.

Taffel, R. (1991a) *Parenting by Heart*. Reading, MA: Addison-Wesley.

Taffel, R. (1991b) 'How to talk with kids', *The Family Therapy Networker*, 15 (4): 38–46, 68–70.

Taffel, R. (1995) 'Honoring the everyday', *The Family Therapy Networker*, 19 (6): 25–8, 56.

Taffel, R. (1996) 'The second family', *The Family Therapy Networker*, 20 (3): 36–45.

Taffel, R. (1998) 'Getting through to difficult parents', workshop at Family Therapy Network Symposium. Washington, D.C.

Taffel, R. and Master, R. (1990) 'Is briefer better?', *The Family Therapy Networker*, 14 (2): 50–56.

Thayer, L. (1982) 'A person-centered approach to family therapy', in A.M Horne and M.M. Ohlsen (eds), *Family Therapy and Counseling*. Ithaca, IL: Peacock.

Thorne, B.F. (1992) *Carl Rogers*. London: Sage.

Titelman, P. (1987) *The Therapist's Own Family: Toward the Differentiation of Self*. Northvale, NJ: Jason Aronson.

Visher, E.B. and Visher, J.S. (1979) *Stepfamilies: A Guide to Working with Stepparents and Stepchildren*. New York: Brunner/Mazel.

Visher, E.B. and Visher, J.S. (1987) *Old Loyalties, New Ties: Therapeutic Strategies with Step-families*. New York: Brunner/Mazel.

Walters, M. (1984) 'Coming of age: reflections on the journey', *The Family Therapy Networker*, 8 (4): 48–50.

Warner, M. (1983) 'Soft meaning and sincerity in the family system', *Family Process*, 22: 522–35.

Warner, M. (1989) 'Empathy and strategy in the family system', *Person Centered Review*, 4 (3): 324–44.

Whitaker, C.A. (1990) 'A day with Carl Whitaker'. Workshop in San Diego, CA.

Whitaker, C.A. and Keith, D.V. (1981) 'Symbolic experiential family therapy', in A.S. Gurman and D.P. Kniskern (eds), *Handbook of Family Therapy*. New York: Brunner/Mazel. pp. 187–226.

Whitaker, C.A. and Napier, A.Y. (1978) *The Family Crucible*. New York: Harper and Row.

White, M. and Epston, D. (1990) *Narrative Means to Therapeutic Ends*. New York: Norton.

Williamson, D.D. (1978) 'New life at the graveyard: a method of therapy for individuation from a dead former parent', *Journal of Marriage and Family Counseling*, 4 (1): 93–101.

Wiltburger, A. (1985) 'Gender and Communication', Living Now Institute, Center for Studies of the Person, La Jolla, CA.

Wood, J.K. (1995) 'The person-centered approach: toward an understanding of its implications', *The Person Centered Journal*, 2 (2): 18–36.

Zimring, F.M. (1988) 'Attaining mastery: the shift from the "me" to the "I"', *Person Centered Review*, 3 (2): 165–76.

Zimring, F.M. (1995) 'A new explanation for the beneficial results of client centered therapy: the possibility of a new paradigm', *The Person Centered Journal*, 2 (2): 36–48.

Index